Noom Diet

Discover the Last Weight Loss Program You'll Ever Need | Quick and Tasty Recipes to Boost your Metabolism and Quickly Burn Stubborn Fat

Legal & Disclaimer

The information contained in this book and its contents is not designed to replace or take the place of any form of medical or professional advice; and is not meant to replace the need for independent medical, financial, legal or other professional advice or services, as may be required. The content and information in this book has been provided for educational and entertainment purposes only.

The content and information contained in this book has been compiled from sources deemed reliable, and it is accurate to the best of the Author's knowledge, information and belief. However, the Author cannot guarantee its accuracy and validity and cannot be held liable for any errors and/or omissions. Further, changes are periodically made to this book as and when needed. Where appropriate and/or necessary, you must consult a professional (including but not limited to your doctor, attorney, financial advisor or such other professional advisor) before using any of the suggested remedies, techniques, or information in this book.

Upon using the contents and information contained in this book, you agree to hold harmless the Author from and against any damages, costs, and expenses, including any legal fees potentially resulting from the application of any of the information provided by this book. This disclaimer applies to any loss, damages or injury caused by the use and application, whether directly or indirectly, of any advice or information presented, whether for breach of contract, tort, negligence, personal injury, criminal intent, or under any other cause of action.

You agree to accept all risks of using the information presented inside this book.

You agree that by continuing to read this book, where appropriate and/or necessary, you shall consult a professional (including but not limited to your doctor, attorney, or financial advisor or such other advisor as needed) before using any of the suggested remedies, techniques, or information in this book.

Table of Contents

INTRODUCTION 6

   WHAT YOU WILL FIND IN THIS BOOK 6

   WHO SHOULD READ THIS BOOK 7

CHAPTER 1: THE NOOM DIET 8

   WHAT THIS DIET IS ALL ABOUT 8

   HOW DOES IT WORK 8

   WHO CAN FOLLOW NOOM DIET 9

   HOW MUCH DOES IT COST TO FOLLOW 10

   BENEFITS OF NOOM DIET 10

      Focus on calories 10

      Offers a dedicated trainer 10

      Encourages behavior change 10

      Offers flexibility in food intake 11

CHAPTER 2: WHAT CAN I EAT? 12

   GREEN FOOD 12

   YELLOW FOOD 13

   RED FOOD 13

CHAPTER 3: CHOOSE YOUR GOAL 15

   GET FIT 15

   LOSE WEIGHT 15

   THE DIFFERENCE BETWEEN THE 2 PLANS 17

   HOW MUCH CALORIES? 19

   MACROS 19

CHAPTER 4: THE NOOM APP 22

   DO I REALLY NEED THE APP? 22

   HOW TO GET THE NOOM APP 23

   HOW TO USE THE NOOM APP 24

CHAPTER 5: CALORIC DENSITY 26

   WHAT IS CALORIC DENSITY? 26

   THE FOOD SYSTEM AT NOOM 27

   FOCUS ON NUTRIENT DENSITY 27

CHAPTER 6: RECIPES IDEAS 29

BREAKFAST RECIPES 30

   GREEK YOGURT BREAKFAST PARFAITS WITH ROASTED GRAPES 30

   POMEGRANATE CHERRY SMOOTHIE BOWL 31

   QUICKIE HONEY NUT GRANOLA 32

   MASHED CHICKPEA, FETA, AND AVOCADO TOAST 34

Baked Ricotta with Pears 35

Breakfast Polenta 36

Scrambled Eggs with Goat Cheese and Roasted Peppers 37

Fruit Bulgur Breakfast Bowl 38

Italian Breakfast Bruschetta 39

Marinara Eggs with Parsley 41

SNACK RECIPES **43**

Bruschetta with Artichoke Hearts and Parmesan 43

Baba Ghanoush 44

Classic Hummus 45

Caponata 47

Easy Toasted Almonds 49

Dolmathes 50

Flavourful Calamari with Oranges 51

Fiery Red Whipped Feta 53

Flavourful Saffron Caulipeas 54

Flavourful Green-Black Olives 55

LUNCH RECIPES **56**

Grilled Chicken Salad with Fennel, Orange, and Raisins 56

Provençal Vegetable Soup 58

Classic Niçoise Chicken 60

Tunisian Turnovers with Tuna, Egg and Tomato 61

Fish and Spinach Gratin 63

Calamari with Herb and Rice Stuffing 64

Grilled Lemon-Herb Chicken and Avocado Salad 66

Tomato Salad with Grilled Halloumi and Herbs 68

The Eggplant Pizza 69

Salmon Bowl with Farro, Black Beans and Tahini Dressing 70

DINNERS RECIPES **72**

Harrisa Potato Salad 72

Greek Lemon Chicken Soup 73

Walnut-Rosemary Crusted Salmon 75

Greek Yogurt Chicken Salad Stuffed Peppers 76

Greek Salad Nachos 77

Caprese Stuffed Portobello Mushrooms 78

Chicken in Tomato-Balsamic Pan Sauce 79

Greek Chicken with Lemon Vinaigrette and Roasted Spring Vegetables 80

Caprese Chicken Hasselback style 82

Chicken Souvlaki Kebabs with Couscous 83

VEGAN/VEGETARIAN RECIPES **85**

Grilled Vegetable and Feta Cheese Salad 85

Dumplings 87

Garlic & Vegetable Calzone 89

Roasted Brussels Sprouts...90

Cauliflower Parmesan Soup 91

Braised Fennel with Lemon 92

Cauliflower Mash 93

Ginger And Butternut Bisque Yum 95

Roasted Broccoli 97

DESSERT RECIPES **98**

Pistachio Ice-Cream..98

Fruity Yogurt Parfait 99

Roasted Pears...100

Chocolate Mousse..102

Tahini Cookies 103

Chocolate Muffins...104

Baklava 106

Blueberry Muffins...107

Cinnamon Apple Chips 108

21-DAY MEAL PLAN **109**

Day 1...109

Day 2...109

Day 3...109

Day 4...109

Day 5...110

Day 6...110

Day 7...110

Day 8...110

Day 9...110

Day 10...111

Day 11...111

Day 12...111

Day 13...111

Day 14...111

Day 15...111

Day 16...112

Day 17...112

Day 18...112

Day 19...112

Day 20...112

Day 21...113

CONCLUSION..**114**

Introduction

What you will find in this book

If you are overweight or obese, then losing weight can improve your self-esteem and help prevent many health problems, including diabetes and heart disease. Dieting has become a common practice in our society, and almost 50 percent of Americans have engaged in some kind of dieting activity. These days, most people know that eating healthy food and exercising are essential parts of any weight loss plan.

However, while many people try different kinds of diets, most give up before they reach their goal. According to one survey, only one in twenty people who join commercial weight loss programs are said to reach their goal weight. Even after initial success, most tend to regain weight after some time.

Why do they fail to lose weight? Most fad diets require calorie restriction, which means drastically cutting down on the amount of food consumed each day. Others require limiting certain food groups in their meal. The basic concept of a diet is to burn more calories than you take in, or at least eat as much as you burn. It sounds easy, but it is not that simple to do in reality. Concentrating on counting calories or excluding certain food groups can be highly stressful and deflect weight loss efforts.

Furthermore, after reaching your desired weight, maintaining that weight for extended periods is more difficult because it requires exercising discipline and increasing its strength over time. Most people can't go more than a few days without succumbing to temptation. You may lose weight in the short term, but your chance of keeping it off for five years or more is very low.

If you have repeatedly tried to lose weight but have never been successful, or you lose weight but then gain it, you need to look further than just your food consumption and exercising - there must be something else holding you back.

A lot of things can trigger food cravings, such as stress, boredom, lack of sleep, change in age, and more. To better understand the reasons behind failed diets, it is vital to understand not just your bodily reaction, but also your mental state and environment.

Good health depends not only on the body but on your mind. You need to consider both physical and mental health and a balance of the mind and body for your holistic health. Likewise, it's essential to take care of both your mind and body to lose weight and to live a healthy life. Thus, learning how to achieve mind and body connection is essential.

Generally speaking, we tend to think of our body and mind as two different systems, and we believe they function separately. In fact, the mind and body are connected through neural pathways made up of neurotransmitters, hormones, and chemicals. Our thoughts, feelings, beliefs, and attitudes can positively or negatively affect our body's functioning.

By focusing more on mental state and using this increased awareness, you can guide your mind to change your lifestyle and eating habits. By staying consciously aware of your physical and emotional sensations while eating, you can succeed in achieving a healthy lifestyle.

Who should read this book

Thinking of shedding some pounds? Noom diet is what you need .

Thinking about whether the Noom Diet is directly for you?

The Noom Diet may simply be the eating regimen that you're searching for. Finding an eating routine that functions admirably for you is significant. It is an eating regimen that has been around for some time however numerous individuals aren't exactly certain precisely what it involves. This guide can help separate it for you with the goal that you know precisely what's in store on the Noom Diet.

In this guide, you'll be getting the hang of everything that you have to think pretty much all that the Noom Diet involves.

Chapter 1: The Noom Diet

what this diet is all about

Noom is a kind of diet that aims to encourage people to practice healthy eating habit, this type of diet do not want you to give up food you like to eat. This diet entails making long terms changes that will assist you to lose weight, this diet was develop by psychologist, nutritionist to assist people to lose weight.

This diet focus on practicing long term effect and it is not like other form of diet which involves losing weight base on fast approach on a short period of time by avoiding certain food.

Individual is expected to pay a fee of $ 59 each month or they can pay a fee of $ 200 annually so that they can have access to the application.

This diet helps you to take control of your weight, exercise, blood pressure and your blood sugar level. The process begins when you sign in to the application and you will be asked series of question that will help the team of noom to assist you.

The noom team can also assist people that are suffering from type 1 and type 2 diabetes. They also assist people from becoming overweight as well as assist obese individual from becoming diabetes.

How does it work

Noom uses an algorithm that depends on your health targets. It helps analyze an individual's daily calorie intake. It makes a personalized diet plan with a focus on different colors of food and nutrition. The program is specially adapted to your lifestyle. It estimates your daily calorie needs based on your age, height, and current weight and activity levels.

There is no limit to your food intake, but Noom diet focuses on takingg low-calorie foods for faster weight loss. Studies have found that a low-calorie diet that includes lots of fruits, vegetables, and low-fat dairy products helps you lose 1 to 2 pounds a week (7).

The Noom app has unique color codes that classify foods based on their caloric content. Green color-coded foods have fewer calories, while those with yellow and red color codes have moderate and higher calories, respectively.

The application assigns color codes to foods based on the food record. One study showed that people who are aware enough to record their daily calorie intake lose significantly more weight compared to those who monitor their meals and activities less frequently. The application also has SOS motivation plans that indicate warning signs, danger zones, and reaction signs. The warning signs describe what you should and shouldn't do when your motivation starts to decline. The danger zones show a red flag that reminds you that you have lost your daily log several times. Reaction signals help you start your milestones.

Who can follow noom diet

Diet plans are not simply lists of foods you should or shouldn't eat. Diet plans cover what to eat, how much to eat, when to eat and what to use to supplement the food you're eating. Many diet plans also cover exercise and an increasing number includes mindfulness.

Adopting a new diet means making a change, but before deciding on the diet you should be clear on the change you want to make, why you want to make it and whether the change would be one for the better.

The vast majority of people embark on a new diet for one of the following reasons:

1. They want to lose weight.

2. They want to control a disease or condition without resorting to medication.

3. They're feeling the first signs of aging and want to improve their longevity.

The desire to lose weight is by far the least controversial. Since the obesity epidemic, it seems that almost everyone is classed as overweight to some extent, but does that matter if you are healthy and comfortable? The Healthy At Every Size movement says "no" and goes further, saying that dieting does not necessarily produce a healthy outcome. Many dieters suffer from depression and even body dysmorphia before they begin and these are conditions that can be exacerbated by calorie restriction. Is it right, in that case, to embark on a diet at all?

How much does it cost to follow

The Noom Diet is a reasonable weight reduction plan that anybody can do.

After you choose to join the Noom Diet, you'll have the option to get to it free for the initial 14 days to verify that you're content with your choice. From that point onward, you'll be charged $ 49.95 every month to proceed with the program.

There is no responsibility to stay aware of the program and you can drop it anytime. Obviously the more you remain on the eating routine, the more advantages, conference and results that you'll get.

Benefits of Noom diet

The Noom diet is a health-based app that focuses on a long-term plan for losing weight. It has numerous benefits.

Focus on calories

The Noom app indicates the number of caloric of different foods. Restricting calories is one of the best approaches to losing weight. A diet low in carbohydrates, calories, and fats (along with a low glycemic index) helps prevent weight gain and promotes weight maintenance.

Most fruits and vegetables are not only low in calories but also high in fiber. They also tend to have a moderate glycemic index and promote satiety. Thus, they can assist in weight loss.

Offers a dedicated trainer

A dedicated coach always brings many changes in an individual's patterns of behavior and lifestyle. A study in the Journal of Medical Internet Research showed that providing trainers/ coaches as part of a weight loss program increased user engagement and led to a positive change in body mass index (BMI).

The Noom app offers an interactive interface with participants-coaches messages, group messages, and daily challenges that help change behavior for long-term health and weight loss.

Encourages behavior change

Healthy behavior change promotes weight loss. Randomized clinical trials in 122 adults showed that behavioral modification helped weight loss better than mere weight loss pills. Data on long-term effects are limited.

The Noom diet plan is a healthy behavioral change and lifestyle intervention program that guarantees individualized motivational and behavioral changes. The changes are supervised by Noom Coaches, the support groups, and psychology-based content. They ensure a constant supply of motivational blog posts that help users stay up to date and healthily lose weight.

Offers flexibility in food intake

Many programs try to reduce food intake to influence weight loss. But the Noom diet follows the opposite approach. It offers total flexibility in the choice of foods from the green, yellow, and red groups, with a primary focus on portion control.

Red group foods are rich in energy, but the Noom diet plan did not omit them. Eliminating desserts and sweets make a diet plan becomes monotonous. Therefore, the Noom diet plan allows you to eat them but in small amounts to satisfy your cravings for sweets.

You can also add an innovative touch to your healthy foods by following Noom's recipes.

Chapter 2: What can i eat?

Green Food

The green list is what you have to focus most of your attention on. Foods in the green category are those with the lowest caloric density or contain many other very healthy nutrients that are very good for healthy eating and your diet.

As you would expect, these are predominantly green vegetables, whole grains, some fruits, and berries, as well as some dairy products.

These are ideal foods to focus on and plan throughout the day to satiate you and avoid the dreaded pangs of hunger while losing weight.

Fruits: banana, apple, orange, pineapple, strawberry, melons, peaches, and blueberry.

Vegetables: green salad, Brussels sprouts, zucchini, carrot, cherry tomato, cucumber, tomato, onion, broccoli, and peas

Starchy foods: Potato, sweet potato, corn, squashes, and beet.

Dairy and dairy products: non-fat Greek yogurt, skim milk, and non-fat cheese slice

Dairy alternatives: tofu, cashew milk, and almond milk.

Whole grains: oatmeal, brown rice, grain tortilla, wheat bread, grain pita, grain pasta, and grain cereals

Beverages: unsweetened tea or coffee.

Yellow Food

This category is slightly denser in calories, and you should only have a moderate amount of them in your diet plan.

These yellow foods are also a little less nutritionally beneficial, although many yellow foods have health benefits and can fill you up, you won't get as many benefits from them.

What's excellent about color coding is that you can search for a group of foods and then choose greens instead of yellows for healthy eating.

Lean meats: skinless chicken, turkey, lean cuts of beef/ pork, and lamb.

Seafood: tuna, scallops, and salmon, tilapia.

Dairy and dairy products: low-fat cottage cheese, low-fat milk, low-fat cheese, and Greek yogurt

Dairy alternative: tempeh

Legumes: baked beans, pinto beans, black beans, and hummus.

Grains: white rice, couscous, quinoa, quiche, white bread, pita bread, English muffins, and seitan

Beverages: diet soda and beer

Others: Guacamole, tempeh.

Red Food

These are food lists you should try to avoid or at least keep your portion size as small as possible. These red foods have more caloric density or have very little nutritional value.

In most cases, they are the ones that prevent people from eating healthy and reach the goals to lose weight.

Meats: hot dog, ham, red meat, sausage, salami, fried meat, bacon, and hamburgers.

Nuts and seeds: chia seeds, nuts, flaxseeds, and hemp seeds

Nuts butter: peanut butter and other kinds of nut butter

Desserts and sweets: chocolate, cookies, pastries, chocolate cake, and energy and snack bars

Dairy and dairy products: full-fat cheese, feta cheese, and whole milk

Snacks: potato chips and French fries

Dressings: mayonnaise and ranch dressing

Fats: butter

Sugars: honey and white sugar.

Beverages: Wine and strained juices.

Chapter 3: Choose Your Goal

Get fit

The Noom project emphasizes regular movement, but not so much strenuous exercise. The app can be used to track movement using a pedometer and one thing the coach will do is encourage you to work on one or other aspect of your weight loss plan, either what you eat or how much your exercise. Walking is the Noom exercise of choice and of course there are many choices. You might walk to school, walk to the office, take the stairs instead of the elevator or simply park your car further from the office door to increase the number of steps you take each day.

A great deal of staying healthy as you age is about staying mobile. As you get older, for example, objects can seem heavier than they were before, it can be far more difficult to lift your arms above your head than it used to be and your body tends to stiffen up.

The good news is that research shows mobility will return if you take up exercise, even if you've never exercised before, however the Noom diet, being aimed primarily at millennials, is more concerned with the effect of exercise on calorie intake. Hence, if you can increase the number of calories you use in a day, your coach may suggest that you can increase your calorie allowance for food.

Lose Weight

When setting out on any diet, it's important to assess your current situation before determining how much, if any, weight should be lost. This is not as simple or straightforward as might be supposed since even within the medical profession there is debate as to the best way to determine whether any specific person is obese or not and no real agreement as to what an ideal weight should be. For example, conventional measurements like Body Mass Index (BMI) make it easy to classify large, muscular people within the obese category.

Did you know Vin Diesel was overweight? Did you know Dwayne Johnson was obese? Yes, at a towering 6' 5" tall and weighing 270lbs, "The Rock" can calculate his BMI and be told to lose weight just like the rest of us.

Body Mass Index is known to be less accurate than other factors when it comes to predicting our general health and susceptibility to disease. Waist size, for example, measures the amount of body fat in a crucial area of the body and many researchers feel this is a better indicator of risk for heart disease. A simple desire to live a healthier life may be one of the best possible reasons to adopt a new eating plan.

If weight loss isn't your main reason for adopting a new diet, you may simply want to eat more healthily. This often happens in reaction to medical tests.

One extremely contentious area is in the recommended diet for diabetes. If you aim to avoid a need for medication, it is important to understand your condition and learn why what you eat makes a difference. Your dietary aim will be to avoid spikes in your blood sugar and this means careful control of your food intake. Your intake of carbs has the greatest effect on your blood sugar levels.

The National Institute for Health, for example, recommends a low-fat diet for those with diabetes. The diet is well known and publicized as a treatment, yet the number of people with diabetes continues to increase.

Many writers also point out that the first low-fat guidelines were published in 1977, a date which is also seen as the start of the obesity epidemic. Is this a coincidence, or are we simply continuing to treat diabetes with a diet we know doesn't work? Despite the increased availability of medication to lower blood pressure and cholesterol the death rate from CVD (cardiovascular disease), for example, continues to increase.

If this is the case for you, consider that studies of the "Blue-Zones" show there are many other factors at work in the lifestyle of "blue-zone" dwellers. It is more important to enjoy a healthy life than a long one. A lack of stress, a slower pace of life, regular exercise and engagement with a supportive community all seem to be important. If your major motivation in dieting is disease resistance, consider the research before jumping one way or another.

Government guidelines (and hence official medical advice) is clear. A low-fat diet is recommended, for example, for those at risk of developing heart disease. When these guidelines were published, scientists believed that saturated fat was a significant cause of heart disease.[2] Patients were discouraged from eating dairy products as a whole (including eggs) but modern research disagrees. Several studies have found no link at all between saturated fat and the prevalence of heart problems. As one paper from 2012 put it: "Results and conclusions about saturated fat intake in relation to cardiovascular disease, from leading advisory committees, do not reflect the available scientific literature."[3]

This is not new. Across the years "good" health has been given as the reason for several behaviors we now know to be harmful. Smoking, for example, was promoted as a cure for coughs and irritated throats and individuals in white coats were widely used in adverts to promote their 'health benefits'.[4] The need to develop or improve your musculature is another good reason to adopt a new way of eating and it's interesting to see that at this point the "diet" industry diverges.

While weight-loss diets are all about what you can't do, muscle gain diets are all about what you can. Muscle enthusiasts take things in a very different direction, creating protein shakes and adding to their meals rather than cutting calories and coping with depression.

Appearance can be one of the better reasons to adopt a new diet and it's important to note that improved appearance does not necessarily involve weight-loss. You may choose to eat more vitamin and mineral-rich foods (for example) as a way of improving poor skin or hair, either in answer to a health problem (such as acne) or simply to improve your self-confidence.

The difference between the 2 plans

The Noom diet plan has many similarities with other diet regimes. Like the Shibboleth Lifestyle (and to some extent Weight Watchers), Noom sees weight loss in context, providing support to the individual, helping them to understand their eating behaviors and make new habits where necessary.

Noom knows that psychology has a great deal to do with weight, though the app's understanding of **being** overweight may be somewhat skewed. One "lesson" suggested avoiding those who thought it was strange if you ate salad. As most overweight women know, disapproving looks from others are far more common when you don't eat a salad than when you do.

Noom works on the basis that all you have to do to lose weight is cut down on your calorie intake. When your body is running normally, it stores excess energy as sugar (short term) and fat (long term), but when you cut back on calories, this stops. Your body knows the food you're eating won't support you and so it pulls energy from your reserves. Short term immediate requirements come from your remaining stored sugar, longer-term requirements come from the fat you already stored.

It sounds simple, doesn't it?

If you've ever been on a diet, you know it's nothing like that easy, no matter what scientists say. You may be determined, for one reason or another, to follow a diet regime, but what comes next can be miserable. You get hungry, cold and irritable. You feel tired and often depressed. If you lose weight it's good, if you don't you'll feel bad. When you don't lose weight it's always your fault; no-one ever seems to consider whether the diet plan doesn't work'. It's only in recent years doctors have admitted, we're not all the same. Diets that work for some may not work for others.

Worst of all, research shows that if you **stay** on a calorie-restricted diet your metabolism adjusts. Weight-loss slows down and even stops. The word used is "plateau," but what it means is that you can't go any further. Your weight stands still.

The moment you weaken, the moment you eat a so-called "normal" meal, that's the moment the weight starts to pile back on and it never stops where it started. You always put on more than you lost.

This is where lifestyle changes are the most important. If your eating habits return to the "norm" your body does the same (and more). If the "norm" is something new, if Noom succeeds in teaching you a healthier way of living, then there is no reason for the body to return to its unhealthy state.

Users of the Noom food app are encouraged to use the app to record what they eat and drink. Is this because Noom's coaches snoop on your food choices and tell you off when you eat too many red foods? Not at all.

Research shows that the simple act of recording what you eat increases weight loss.

"Every day I hear patients say they can't lose weight. This study shows that most people can lose weight if they have the right tools and support," says Keith Bachman, MD, a Kaiser Permanente internist and weight management specialist. "Keeping a food diary doesn't have to be a formal thing. Just the act of scribbling down what you eat on a Post-It note, sending yourself e-mails tallying each meal, or sending yourself a text message will suffice. It's the process of reflecting on what we eat that helps us become aware of our habits, and hopefully change our behavior."

Furthermore, the time taken to log what you eat is proportional to weight loss success.

Although keeping a record of what you eat isn't easy, you have to estimate the amount as well as list the foods themselves, Noom has done as much as it can to make the process painless. If there is something you cook regularly, you can enter it into the app for analysis and future use. If you eat prepared or processed foods (and

18

who doesn't these days), you can use your phone's camera to scan the bar code on the packaging and enter the information that way. In addition to logging your food intake, Noom encourages you to log your weight every day.

Other weight-loss regimes, like weight watchers and the Shibboleth lifestyle, suggest daily weigh-ins are not a good idea. Weight can fluctuate over a day, and the heavier the individual the more it fluctuates (and the more help that individual needs). Women also see a weight fluctuation over their menstrual cycle.

Since depression, and in some cases body dysmorphia are all factors involved with weight problems, common sense dictates that any exacerbation of these conditions is to be avoided. A woman who is already depressed and hungry as a result of her diet is unlikely to feel highly motivated after a weigh-in which shows little progress.

Recent scientific studies[3] disagree[4] with that approach and instead advocate daily weighing as a "useful tool for successful weight management" in our "obesogenic environment" however experts agree that this does not lead to advanced weight loss when added to traditional weight loss programs.

How much calories?

It is easy to talk about healthy choices and good habits, but in order to achieve that it is important to uncover what exactly makes a diet healthy. The Australian Dietary Guidelines defines a healthy diet as eating foods and having dietary patterns, which aim to "promote health and wellbeing, reduce the risk of diet-related conditions, such as high cholesterol, high blood pressure and reduce the risk of chronic diseases such as type-2 diabetes, cardiovascular disease and some types of cancer." According to The Guidelines the type of diet that meets those criteria is a diet that includes a large variety of foods from different food groups, such as large amounts of vegetables, beans and legumes, fruit, grains, lean meats and poultry, fish, eggs, tofu, nuts and seeds and low-fat dairy products. It also states that a healthy diet limits the intake of foods containing high levels of sodium, saturated fats, added sugar and alcohol. In addition to these above mentioned guidelines you should also make sure you eat a diet that meets your calorie needs. If you are a triathlete, runner, swimmer, or cyclist then your calorie requirements are likely to be higher than the average persons and that needs to be accounted for in order to ensure that your body has the proper amount of fuel needed to perform at its best. A high-performance athlete usually requires between 2000-5000 calories daily depending on gender, age, and fitness and activity level.

Macros

The human body needs both macro- and micronutrients on a daily basis to thrive. Micronutrients are vitamins and minerals (and will be covered later), while macronutrients are the big three: Carbohydrates, protein and fats.

These three serve different purposes within the body, and they each provide your body with the fuel it needs to perform and make sure you do not run out of energy half way through.

Carbohydrates

Carbohydrates are found in such foods as fruit, vegetables, beans, legumes, bread, oats and pasta and they help regulate your blood glucose levels and the glycogen levels in the muscles and give you energy. Carbs turn to glucose (blood sugar) in the body and are then used for energy. It is stored as glucose in the liver and muscles where from it releases energy when needed. Carbs can be either simple or complex, referring to how complex their molecular structure is. Complex carbs are the "good" kind of carbs, because they provide and maintain a stable blood glucose level and they contain fibres, vitamins and minerals – unlike simple carbohydrates, which only consists of one or two sugar molecules. The simple carbohydrates are easily turned to energy in the body, as they are very rapidly digested, providing a quick burst of energy. However, they also make the body's blood glucose level unsteady. Your main energy source should be complex carbohydrates from whole plant foods.

Protein

Protein are large molecules that play a role in all cellular processes. It serves a lot of different functions in the body and is key in building and restoring muscle tissue after strenuous activities. It is an important macronutrient for athletes, because of the repeated breakdown of muscle tissue during workouts and competitions. Protein can be found in most foods and you should opt for quality sources such as various beans, tofu, lean meats, poultry, fish, eggs and dairy products.

Fatty acids

Fatty acids are hydrocarbon chains with a tail of carboxylic acid groups. They are hydrophobic, which is why fat and water do not mix. The fatty acids have several important functions in the body including serving as a cellular fuel source and storage of energy within the adipose tissue. There are different types of fats, some beneficial for the body, some harmful. You should opt for the mono- and polyunsaturated fats found in fish, avocado, walnuts, chia and flax seeds, among other foods, and avoid the saturated and trans fatty acids found in heavily processed products and deep-fried foods. Healthy fat sources provide your body with energy and is especially important for athletes doing long-term aerobic performances. For short bouts of exercise and especially for anaerobic activities such as sprinting, carbohydrates are the main energy source, but when you exceed approximately sixty minutes of training without food intake your body will burn up all the stored carbs and will then switch to using fat as an energy source.

Eating a healthy, balanced diet will ensure that you get enough energy to fuel your body during workouts or competitions, but there are other reasons why it is important to eat healthy. Quite often weight is an important aspect of an athlete's life. Eating a healthy, balanced diet will help regulate your body weight and keep it stable, making it easier to meet your goals.

It is also important to stay hydrated as that will also aid in a well-balanced body. You should aim to consume about three to six ounces of water for every twenty minutes of exercise. Sometimes it's not possible to drink water mid-performance, and in that case it is important to rehydrate post-exercise to maintain a healthy fluid balance in your body and avoid dehydration, which puts your ability to perform in jeopardy. For long bouts of physical exertion there is also a loss of sodium and other minerals through sweating. In order to make up for this loss of minerals you may consider ingesting sports drinks to replenish your stores. They also contain easily absorbed carbohydrates, which are important to refuel after vigorous exercise has left you depleted.

Chapter 4: The Noom App

Do i really need the app?

We know that the Noom app is not designed for dieting per se; it is designed to answer how nutritional and behavioral changes are a factor of health and wellness, and how a healthier lifestyle can affect weight loss. The Noom program, therefore, introduces the concept of "self-efficacy" -- a belief in oneself and in one's capacity to achieve both behavioral and nutritional goals.

There is one important thing that pops up when you first log on to Noom: it is a welcoming message that says, "Noom: Stop dieting. Get life-long results." This welcoming phrase really captures Noom's mission in just 6 words. We can say this phrase alone propels Noom toward navigating a consistent trend from the normal goal of "weight loss" to that of "wellness". If you would like to see how Noom describes its program, see below:

"Noom uses cutting-edge technology to accurately monitor your progress and provide expert advice and analysis to keep you on track. By making the experience relevant to who you are, your goals, and your interactions, we provide a personalized plan that makes a balanced, healthy life attainable and fun."

In a sense, you will be asked to track your meals daily on Noom app. The Noom diet plan provides guidance, motivation, and a structure meant to inspire better eating and healthy lifestyle choices that should last a lifetime.

How to get the Noom App

The signup process with Noom is relatively straightforward. You answer questions, pick a starter plan, hand over your credit card information follow instructions to download the app. For me, this is a major annoyance. Having an app is a convenience, but the best apps can also be used on a laptop and that is not the case with Noom (at the time of writing).

Once signed up, the process begins when you are allocated a calorie level designed to help you achieve your weight goals in a reasonable time. Each day you log your meals and snacks and the amount remaining on your calorie allowance is shown. You can then go to the recipes section where you can search for meals that fit within your allowance.

Your first exercise is to "design your big picture" from three parts you'll identify yourself

1. Your Super Goal. This is something measurable but not necessarily weight-related. Examples given in the app include "**Rocking a bathing suit without breaking a sweat (unless it's really sunny out).**"

2. Your Ultimate Why. This is the result of responding "**why**" several times to the question "what's your goal." For example:

"What's your goal?"

"To lose 10lbs in weight."

" Why?"

This one can be difficult since it seems the answer is obvious. If your ultimate why is "So I can feel confident at my wedding" should Noom point out that weight loss is not required?

Just click the button "yes this inspires and excites me" and you can move on to...

3. How your life will be different.

From the "big picture," you move on to caloric density and the app explains why eating foods with a low cd will help you feel full up for longer.

The next day is all about weight. You're due to "weigh-in" and Noom psychologists know all about the complex relationship between a dieter and their scales. The bottom line is always the same. Information is important. You need to know what your weight is so you can check whether it is going up or down. The same applies to

23

logging food, especially if you can find a pattern relating to the two. You'll also create an S.O.S. Plan to be used when your motivation fails, as demonstrated by your willingness to record your meals and your weight every day. You might ask your Noom support group to send you a text, or a friend might reach out to you or even your spouse to get you back on the path to success.

Next, you'll learn about habits and triggers of different kinds and go through a process to help define yours, but as this is done alone, you may not find it easy to identify. Overeating is a simple one to choose, but finding your triggers was not, for me, as easy as the app seemed to think.

How to use the Noom App

Users of the Noom food app are encouraged to use the app to record what they eat and drink. Is this because Noom's coaches snoop on your food choices and tell you off when you eat too many red foods? Not at all.

Research shows that the simple act of recording what you eat increases weight loss.

"Every day I hear patients say they can't lose weight. This study shows that most people can lose weight if they have the right tools and support," says Keith Bachman, MD, a Kaiser Permanente internist and weight management specialist. "Keeping a food diary doesn't have to be a formal thing. Just the act of scribbling down what you eat on a Post-It note, sending yourself e-mails tallying each meal, or sending yourself a text message will suffice. It's the process of reflecting on what we eat that helps us become aware of our habits, and hopefully change our behavior."

Furthermore, the time taken to log what you eat is proportional to weight loss success.

Although keeping a record of what you eat isn't easy, you have to estimate the amount as well as list the foods themselves, Noom has done as much as it can to make the process painless. If there is something you cook regularly, you can enter it into the app for analysis and future use. If you eat prepared or processed foods (and who doesn't these days), you can use your phone's camera to scan the bar code on the packaging and enter the information that way. In addition to logging your food intake, Noom encourages you to log your weight every day.

Recent scientific studie disagree with that approach and instead advocate daily weighing as a "useful tool for successful weight management" in our "obesogenic environment" however experts agree that this does not lead to advanced weight loss when added to traditional weight loss programs.

Below are some features that enable Noom to work effectively for users:

24

Psychological Therapy: Noom deals with user psychology or mental components to help solve health and weight challenges. Other app-based diets lack this -- their programs do not deal with the thoughts which are the root of the problem. Noom's approach assists users to fight their emotional and mental challenges between where they are and where exactly they want to be.

Food Strategy: Selecting food on Noom deals with a calorie density strategy. Noom coaches use this strategy to tackle nutritional problems. Noom categorizes foods into three categories: green, yellow, and red, in accordance with the calorie densities. With these, users understand what makes up the food they eat in order to make healthier choices daily.

Mailing: Since you can access the program on their app, Noom makes mailing available for you. This will keep you updated and notified whenever you have a notification from either your coach or group mates.

Tracking: There is a feature on the app that helps you track all your intake meals. This gives users simple tasks daily, including brief health lessons.

Feedback: Users have a better understanding of food choices and portions from the feedback they receive from their previous food intake.

Health Education: In the form of health education, the Noom program has weekly lessons that are incorporated into courses. This helps users understand their health status better than they can ever imagine.

Chapter 5: Caloric Density

what is caloric density?

When it comes to weight loss, people have focused on calorie counting by burning more calories than what they eat. Counting calories used to be the major focus in most diet programs, but it's not enough for sustainable weight loss. Calorie-restricted diets can only perform their functions within a short term -- most dieters regain their lost weight after a short time. While "eating less" is the main strategy for most other diet programs, Noom's principal food strategy is "eating smart".

Eating only low-calorie foods can leave you feeling hungry and unfulfilled not long after your meals. If you could feel full with less calorie intake, it would help you manage your weight more effectively. To become full and stay full without eating a large number of calories, you must incorporate foods that support your body's need to feel full. Therefore, eating smart is more important than eating less.

"Calorie Density" is one of the most important concepts you should be familiar with when working on the Noom diet for healthful eating and lifelong weight management. By understanding how Calorie Density works, you will be able to not just lose weight but improve your diet. Research shows that the amount of food you eat has a greater effect on how full you feel than the number of calories in the food. By using calorie density, if you choose foods that have fewer calories per bite, your portion size can grow without increasing the overall calorie count. That means you can eat more and feel full on fewer calories. For example, for 50 calories you could eat one cup (150 grams) of strawberries or 1/ 10 cup of raisins. Therefore, you can consume a larger portion of a low-calorie density food than a high-calorie density food for the same number of calories. Research studies have also shown that diets based on low calorie-density foods tend to be healthier and more effective for weight management.

Calorie Density (also called Energy Density) is a measure of the calorie content in a given volume or weight of food -- in other words, the total amount of energy provided per unit measure of food. It is usually measured as calories per 100 grams (3.5 ounces) of food.

Calorie Density = Calories per serving/Grams per serving

The food system at noom

Knowing what to eat is always important when it comes to figuring out healthy weight loss. Although Noom focuses more on the psychological aspects of eating, there is an important strategy behind our food choices and how to slowly change old habits.

Noom provides a nutritional method as part of a comprehensive weight loss program. It involves knowing what to eat, how much to take in, and following an eating guideline that suits your lifestyle.

Noom specifies each food item categorized by the caloric value in their database, and managing your calorie goal is made simple for you. Food strategy is so important with Noom if you are looking for a way to achieve your long-term weight-loss and management goal. Let us look at two keys that can guide users to achieve this:

A "No-food-off-limit" Approach

Most weight loss programs restrict the selection of foods you will be allowed to eat while on the program. With Noom, all foods are allowed -- absolutely no foods are off-limits. Noom focuses on moderation and portion control based on a food-specific categorization. A balanced lifestyle is what you will make strenuous efforts for. Noom has a unique point value that is encoded in colors and this guides Noom users to choose their daily food choices and the right one to eat from the three color categories.

Focus on nutrient density

It focus on calorie density, this has to deal with the measure of the amount of calories a particular food give when compare with its volume or weight, this diet classify food into three types which is the green, yellow and red this is base on the concentration and calories density.

Foods that have highest concentration of nutrient and lowest calorie density are called the green, and then follow by yellow and red. The red have lowest concentration of nutrient but highest calorie density.

Red food have big amount of calories in small portion of food, the green food are rich in fiber and water and they are low in fat. High calorie food provides sugar or fat to the body but they are not rich in fiber and water. Foods that have low calorie are good for weight loss.

Chapter 6: Recipes ideas

Breakfast recipes

Greek Yogurt Breakfast Parfaits with Roasted Grapes

Servings: 4

Total time: 30 minutes

Ingredients

1½ pounds seedless grapes (about 4 cups)

1 tablespoon extra-virgin olive oil

2 cups 2% plain Greek yogurt

½ cup chopped walnuts

4 teaspoons honey

Directions

1.Place a large, rimmed baking sheet in the oven. Preheat the oven to 450°F with the pan inside.

2.Wash the grapes and remove from the stems. Dry on a clean kitchen towel, and put in a bowl. Drizzle with the oil, and toss to coat.

3.Carefully remove the hot pan from the oven, and pour the grapes onto the pan. Bake for 20 to 23 minutes, until slightly shriveled, stirring once halfway through. Remove the baking sheet from the oven and cool on a wire rack for 5 minutes.

4.While the grapes are cooling, assemble the parfaits by spooning the yogurt into four bowls or tall glasses. Top each bowl or glass with 2 tablespoons of walnuts and 1 teaspoon of honey.

5.When the grapes are slightly cooled, top each parfait with a quarter of the grapes. Scrape any accumulated sweet grape juice onto the parfaits and serve.

Prep tip: You can also roast the grapes still on their stems. Place them on the hot baking sheet, and use a basting brush to brush them with olive oil. After baking and cooling, remove the grapes from their stems, or serve them still on the stems on a cheese board like our **Fruit, Veggie, and Cheese Board**.

Pomegranate Cherry Smoothie Bowl

Servings: 5

Total time: 20 minutes

Ingredients

1 (20-ounce) bag frozen dark sweet cherries

1 cups 3% plain Greek yogurt,

1/3 cup juice

1/2 cup 2% milk

2 teaspoon vanilla

¾ teaspoon ground cinnamon

5 ice

½ cup pistachios

1/2 cup pomegranate seeds

Directions

1.Put cherries, , pomegranate, yogurt juice, milk, vanilla, cinnamon and ice cubes in a blender. Purée until thoroughly mixed and smooth. You'll want the mixture bit thicker than the anormal smoothie, but not so thick you can't pour it. If the smoothie is too thick, add another few tablespoons of milk; if it's too thin, add another few tablespoon yogurt

2.Pour the smoothie into four bowls. Top each with 2 tablespoons of pistachios and 2 tablespoons of pomegranate seeds, and serve immediately if possible

Ingredient tip: You can buy packaged pomegranate seeds—also called arils—in the, we'd also encourage you to try buying the whole fruit when they're in season.

Quickie Honey Nut Granola

Servings: 6

Total time: 30 minutes

Ingredients

2½ cups regular rolled oats

⅓ cup coarsely chopped almonds

⅛ teaspoon kosher or sea salt

½ teaspoon ground cinnamon

½ cup chopped dried apricots

2 tablespoons ground flaxseed

¼ cup honey

¼ cup extra-virgin olive oil

2 teaspoons vanilla extract

Directions

1.Preheat the oven to 325°F. Line a large, rimmed baking sheet with parchment paper.

2.In a large skillet, combine the oats, almonds, salt, and cinnamon. Turn the heat to medium-high and cook, stirring often, to toast, about 6 minutes.

3.While the oat mixture is toasting, in a microwave-safe bowl, combine the apricots, flaxseed, honey, and oil. Microwave on high for about 1 minute, or until very hot and just beginning to bubble. (Or heat these ingredients in a small saucepan over medium heat for about 3 minutes.)

4.Stir the vanilla into the honey mixture, then pour it over the oat mixture in the skillet. Stir well.

5.Spread out the granola on the prepared baking sheet. Bake for 15 minutes, until lightly browned. Remove from the oven and cool completely.

6.Break the granola into small pieces, and store in an airtight container in the refrigerator for up to 2 weeks (if it lasts that long!).

Prep tip: When measuring nut butters, honey, maple syrup, or other sticky ingredients, first spray the measuring cup with nonstick cooking spray. Then when you pour (or dump) the sticky ingredients out, they will come right out.

Mashed Chickpea, Feta, and Avocado Toast

Servings: 4

Total time: 15 minutes

Ingredients

1 (15-ounce) can chickpeas, drained and rinsed

1 avocado, pitted

½ cup diced feta cheese (about 2 ounces)

2 teaspoons freshly squeezed lemon juice or 1 tablespoon orange juice

½ teaspoon freshly ground black pepper

4 pieces multigrain toast

2 teaspoons honey

Directions

1.Put the chickpeas in a large bowl. Scoop the avocado flesh into the bowl.

2.With a potato masher or large fork, mash the ingredients together until the mix has a spreadable consistency. It doesn't need to be totally smooth.

3.Add the feta, lemon juice, and pepper, and mix well.

4.Evenly divide the mash onto the four pieces of toast and spread with a knife. Drizzle with honey and serve.

Ingredient tip: If you can't find lower-sodium or no-salt-added canned beans, draining and rinsing a regular can of beans can still reduce the amount of sodium by around 40 percent.

Baked Ricotta with Pears

Servings: 4

Total time: 30 minutes

Ingredients

Nonstick cooking spray

1 (16-ounce) container whole-milk ricotta cheese

2 large eggs

¼ cup white whole-wheat flour or whole-wheat pastry flour

1 tablespoon sugar

1 teaspoon vanilla extract

¼ teaspoon ground nutmeg

1 pear, cored and diced

2 tablespoons water

1 tablespoon honey

Directions

1.Preheat the oven to 400°F. Spray four 6-ounce ramekins with nonstick cooking spray.

2.In a large bowl, beat together the ricotta, eggs, flour, sugar, vanilla, and nutmeg. Spoon into the ramekins. Bake for 22 to 25 minutes, or until the ricotta is just about set. Remove from the oven and cool slightly on racks.

3.While the ricotta is baking, in a small saucepan over medium heat, simmer the pear in the water for 10 minutes, until slightly softened. Remove from the heat, and stir in the honey.

4.Serve the ricotta ramekins topped with the warmed pear.

Prep tip: If you don't have ramekins, use a baking pan and increase the baking time by 10 minutes. You can also heat the pear in the microwave instead of on the stove top. Place the pear and water in a microwave-safe glass bowl and cook on high for 3 minutes. Stir in the honey.

Breakfast Polenta

Servings: 6

Total time: 15 minutes

Ingredients

2 (18-ounce) tubes plain polenta

2¼ to 2½ cups 2% milk, divided

2 oranges, peeled and chopped

½ cup chopped pecans

¼ cup 2% plain Greek yogurt

8 teaspoons honey

Directions

1.Slice the polenta into rounds and place in a microwave-safe bowl. Heat in the microwave on high for 45 seconds.

2.Transfer the polenta to a large pot, and mash it with a potato masher or fork until coarsely mashed. Place the pot on the stove over medium heat.

3.In a medium, microwave-safe bowl, heat the milk in the microwave on high for 1 minute. Pour 2 cups of the warmed milk into the pot with the polenta, and stir with a whisk. Continue to stir and mash with the whisk, adding the remaining milk a few tablespoons at a time, until the polenta is fairly smooth and heated through, about 5 minutes. Remove from the stove.

4.Divide the polenta among four serving bowls. Top each bowl with one-quarter of the oranges, 2 tablespoons of pecans, 1 tablespoon of yogurt, and 2 teaspoons of honey before serving.

Ingredient tip: Instead of the cooked tubed polenta, you can buy medium-ground or coarsely ground cornmeal, which both have the right consistency to make traditional Italian polenta but take longer to cook. Look for the phrase "stone-ground whole corn," which indicates a whole grain. Follow the directions on the package, using a mixture of half milk and half water for the liquid.

Scrambled Eggs with Goat Cheese and Roasted Peppers

Servings: 4

Total time: 15 minutes

Ingredients

1½ teaspoons extra-virgin olive oil

1 cup chopped bell peppers, any color (about 1 medium pepper)

2 garlic cloves, minced (about 1 teaspoon)

6 large eggs

¼ teaspoon kosher or sea salt

2 tablespoons water

½ cup crumbled goat cheese (about 2 ounces)

2 tablespoons loosely packed chopped fresh mint

Directions

1. In a large skillet over medium-high heat, heat the oil. Add the peppers and cook for 5 minutes, stirring occasionally. Add the garlic and cook for 1 minute.

2. While the peppers are cooking, in a medium bowl, whisk together the eggs, salt, and water.

3. Turn the heat down to medium-low. Pour the egg mixture over the peppers. Let the eggs cook undisturbed for 1 to 2 minutes, until they begin to set on the bottom. Sprinkle with the goat cheese.

4. Cook the eggs for about 1 to 2 more minutes, stirring slowly, until the eggs are soft-set and custardy. (They will continue to cook off the stove from the residual heat in the pan.)

5. Top with the fresh mint and serve.

Prep tip: To prevent tough scrambled eggs, cook them low and slow. If you cook on an electric stove, give your burners a few minutes to cool down when you turn down the heat, then place the skillet back on when the burner is truly at a medium-low heat.

Fruit Bulgur Breakfast Bowl

Servings: 6

Total time: 20 minutes

Ingredients

1½ cups uncooked bulgur

2 cups 2% milk

1 cup water

½ teaspoon ground cinnamon

2 cups frozen (or fresh, pitted) dark sweet cherries

8 dried (or fresh) figs, chopped

½ cup chopped almonds

¼ cup loosely packed fresh mint, chopped

Warm 2% milk, for serving (optional)

Directions

1. In a medium saucepan, combine the bulgur, milk, water, and cinnamon. Stir once, then bring just to a boil. Cover, reduce the heat to medium-low, and simmer for 10 minutes or until the liquid is absorbed.

2. Turn off the heat, but keep the pan on the stove, and stir in the frozen cherries (no need to thaw), figs, and almonds. Stir well, cover for 1 minute, and let the hot bulgur thaw the cherries and partially hydrate the figs. Stir in the mint.

3. Scoop into serving bowls. Serve with warm milk, if desired. You can also serve it chilled.

Prep tip: Dried fruit can be cumbersome to chop; the fruit pieces can stick to the knife, forcing you to stop often to remove them. To prevent this, spray your knife with nonstick cooking spray to slice easily through dried fruit.

Italian Breakfast Bruschetta

Servings: 4

Total time: 30 minutes

Ingredients

¼ teaspoon kosher or sea salt

6 cups broccoli rabe, stemmed and chopped (about 1 bunch)

1 tablespoon extra-virgin olive oil

2 garlic cloves, minced (about 1 teaspoon)

1 ounce prosciutto, cut or torn into ½-inch pieces

¼ teaspoon crushed red pepper

Nonstick cooking spray

3 large eggs

1 tablespoon 2% milk

¼ teaspoon freshly ground black pepper

4 teaspoons grated Parmesan or Pecorino Romano cheese

1 garlic clove, halved

8 (¾-inch-thick) slices baguette-style whole-grain bread or 4 slices larger Italian-style whole-grain bread

Directions

1.Bring a large stockpot of water to a boil. Add the salt and broccoli rabe, and boil for 2 minutes. Drain in a colander.

2.In a large skillet over medium heat, heat the oil. Add the garlic, prosciutto, and crushed red pepper, and cook for 2 minutes, stirring often. Add the broccoli rabe and cook for an additional 3 minutes, stirring a few times. Transfer to a bowl and set aside.

3.Place the skillet back on the stove over low heat and coat with nonstick cooking spray.

4.In a small bowl, whisk together the eggs, milk, and pepper. Pour into the skillet. Stir and cook until the eggs are soft scrambled, 3 to 5 minutes. Add the broccoli rabe mixture back to the skillet along with the cheese. Stir and cook for about 1 minute, until heated through. Remove from the heat.

5.Toast the bread, then rub the cut sides of the garlic clove halves onto one side of each slice of the toast. (Save the garlic for another recipe.) Spoon the egg mixture onto each piece of toast and serve.

Ingredient tip: You can swap in chopped spinach for the broccoli rabe. Skip the boiling and just cook the spinach in the skillet for 2 to 3 minutes, as described in step 2.

Marinara Eggs with Parsley

Servings: 6

Total time: 20 minutes

Ingredients

1 tablespoon extra-virgin olive oil

1 cup chopped onion (about ½ medium onion)

2 garlic cloves, minced (about 1 teaspoon)

2 (14.5-ounce) cans Italian diced tomatoes, undrained, no salt added

6 large eggs

½ cup chopped fresh flat-leaf (Italian) parsley

Crusty Italian bread and grated Parmesan or Romano cheese, for serving (optional)

Directions

1.In a large skillet over medium-high heat, heat the oil. Add the onion and cook for 5 minutes, stirring occasionally. Add the garlic and cook for 1 minute.

2.Pour the tomatoes with their juices over the onion mixture and cook until bubbling, 2 to 3 minutes. While waiting for the tomato mixture to bubble, crack one egg into a small custard cup or coffee mug.

3.When the tomato mixture bubbles, lower the heat to medium. Then use a large spoon to make six indentations in the tomato mixture. Gently pour the first cracked egg into one indentation and repeat, cracking the remaining eggs, one at a time, into the custard cup and pouring one into each indentation. Cover the skillet and cook for 6 to 7 minutes, or until the eggs are done to your liking (about 6 minutes for soft-cooked, 7 minutes for harder cooked).

4.Top with the parsley, and serve with the bread and grated cheese, if desired.

Ingredient tip: A can of Italian diced tomatoes is a convenient ingredient to keep in your pantry and typically contains any combination of onion, garlic, basil, and oregano. Look for cans with only 6 grams or less of sugar and no salt added.

Snack recipes

Bruschetta with Artichoke Hearts and Parmesan

Servings: 10

Total time: 30 minutes

Ingredients

1 cup jarred whole baby artichoke hearts packed in water, rinsed and patted dry

1 garlic clove, minced

1 recipe Toasted Bread for Bruschetta

2 ounces Parmesan cheese, 1 ounce grated fine, 1 ounce shaved

2 tablespoons chopped fresh basil

2 tablespoons extra-virgin olive oil, plus extra for serving

2 teaspoons lemon juice

Salt and pepper

Directions

Pulse artichoke hearts, oil, basil, lemon juice, garlic, ¼ teaspoon salt, and ¼ teaspoon pepper using a food processor until coarsely pureed, about 6 pulses, scraping down sides of the container as required. Put in grated Parmesan and pulse to combine, about 2 pulses.

Lay out artichoke mixture uniformly toasts and top with shaved Parmesan. Season with pepper to taste, and sprinkle with extra oil to taste. Serve.

Baba Ghanoush

Servings: 1

Total time: 1 hour 30 minutes

Ingredients

1 small garlic clove, minced

2 eggplants (1 pound each), pricked all over with fork

2 tablespoons extra-virgin olive oil, plus extra for serving

2 tablespoons tahini

2 teaspoons chopped fresh parsley

4 teaspoons lemon juice

Salt and pepper to taste

Directions

Place the oven rack in the centre of the oven and pre-heat your oven to 500 degrees. Place eggplants on a baking sheet coated with aluminium foil and roast, flipping the eggplants every fifteen minutes, until consistently soft when pressed using tongs, forty minutes to one hour. Allow eggplants to cool for 5 minutes over a baking sheet.

Place a colander on top of a container. Slice the top and bottom off each eggplant and slit eggplants along the length. Using spoon, scoop hot pulp into colander (you should have about 2 cups pulp); discard skins. Allow the pulp to drain for about three minutes.

Move drained eggplant to your food processor. Put in tahini, oil, lemon juice, garlic, ¾ teaspoon salt, and ¼ teaspoon pepper. Pulse the mixture until a rough puree is achieved, approximately 8 pulses. Drizzle with salt and pepper to taste.

Move to serving bowl, cover firmly using plastic wrap, put inside your fridge until chilled, about 1 hour. (Dip will keep safely in a fridge for up to 24 hours; bring to room temperature before you serve.) Drizzle with salt and pepper to taste, sprinkle with extra oil to taste, and drizzle with parsley before you serve.

Classic Hummus

Servings: 2

Total time: 50 minutes

Ingredients

¼ cup water

¼ teaspoon ground cumin

½ teaspoon salt

1 (15-ounce) can chickpeas, rinsed

1 small garlic clove, minced

2 tablespoons extra-virgin olive oil, plus extra for serving

3 tablespoons lemon juice

6 tablespoons tahini

45

Pinch cayenne pepper

Directions

Mix water and lemon juice in a small-sized container. In a different container, beat tahini and oil together.

Process chickpeas, garlic, salt, cumin, and cayenne using a food processor until thoroughly ground, approximately fifteen seconds.

Scrape down sides of the container using a rubber spatula. While the machine runs, put in lemon juice mixture gradually. Scrape down sides of the container and carry on processing for about sixty seconds. While the machine runs, put in tahini mixture gradually and process until hummus is smooth and creamy, approximately fifteen seconds, scraping down sides of the container as required.

Move hummus to serving bowl, cover up using plastic wrap, and allow to sit at room temperature until flavours blend, approximately half an hour.

If you wish, you can refrigerate this dish for up to 5 days.

If needed, loosen hummus using 1 tablespoon warm water. Sprinkle with extra oil to taste before you serve.

Caponata

Servings: 3

Total time: 20 minutes

Ingredients

¼ cup chopped fresh parsley

¼ cup pine nuts, toasted

¼ cup raisins

1/3 cup red wine vinegar, plus extra for seasoning

½ teaspoon salt

¾ cup V8 juice

1 celery rib, chopped fine

1 large eggplant (1½ pounds), cut into ½-inch cubes

2 tomato, cored

2 red bell pepper, stemmed, seeded, and chopped fine

2 small onion, chopped fine (½ cup)

1 teaspoons anchovy fillets (2 to 3 fillets)

1 tablespoons minced black olives

3 tablespoons brown sugar

3 tablespoons olive oil

Directions

Toss eggplant with salt in a pan. Thoroughly coat the full surface of big microwave-safe plate using double layer of coffee filters and lightly spray using vegetable oil spray. Lay out eggplant in a uniform layers. Microwave until eggplant is dry and shriveled to one-third of its original size, about eight to fifteen minutes (Do not let it brown). Move eggplant instantly to paper towel–lined plate.

In the meantime, beat V8 juice, vinegar, sugar, parsley, and anchovies together in medium bowl. Mix tomato, raisins and olives in

Heat 1 tablespoon oil in 12-inch non-stick frying pan on moderate to high heat until it starts to shimmer. Put in eggplant and cook, stirring intermittently, until edges become browned, about four to eight minutes, adding 1 teaspoon more oil if pan seems to be dry; move to a container.

Put in remaining 2 teaspoons oil to empty frying pan and heat on moderate to high heat until it starts shimmering. Put in celery, bell peppe and onion and cook while stirring intermittently, till they become tender and edges are spotty brown, 6 to 8 minutes.

Decrease heat to moderate to low and mix in eggplant and V8 juice mixture. Bring to simmer and cook until V8 juice becomes thick and covers the vegetables, four to eight minutes. Move to serving bowl and allow to cool to room temperature. (Caponata can be refrigerated safely in a fridge for up to seven days; bring to room temperature before you serve.)

Drizzle some with extra vinegar to taste and pine nuts before you serve.

Easy Toasted Almonds

Servings: 2

Total time: 15 minutes

Ingredients

¼ teaspoon pepper

1 tablespoon extra-virgin olive oil

1 teaspoon salt

2 cups skin-on raw whole almonds

Directions

Heat oil in 12-inch non-stick frying pan on moderate to high heat until it barely starts shimmering. Put in almonds, salt, and pepper and decrease the heat to moderate to low. Cook, stirring frequently, until almonds become aromatic and their colour becomes somewhat deep, approximately eight minutes.

Move almonds to plate coated using paper towels and allow to cool before you serve.

If you wish, you can store Almonds at room temperature for up to 5 days.

Dolmathes

Servings: 24

Total time: 1 hour 40 minutes

Ingredients

¼ cup chopped mint

⅓ cup chopped dill

¾ cup short-grain white rice

1 jar grape leaves

1 large onion chopped fine

1½ tablespoons grated lemon zest

2 tablespoons extra-virgin olive oil, plus extra for serving

Salt and pepper

Directions

Keep 26 grape leaves, approximately 6 inches in diameter; save for later rest of the leaves. Bring 7 cups water to boil in a saucepan. Put in grape leaves and cook for about seventy seconds. Gently drain leaves and move to a container of cold water to cool, about 5 minutes. Drain again, then move leaves to plate and cover loosely using plastic wrap.

Heat oil in now-empty saucepan over medium heat until it starts shimmering. Put in onion and ½ teaspoon salt and cook till they become tender and lightly browned, 5 to 7 minutes. Put in rice and cook stir frequently, until grain edges begin to turn translucent, three minutes. Mix in ¾ cup water and bring to boil. Decrease heat to low, cover, and simmer gently until rice becomes soft but still firm in center and water has been absorbed, 10 to 12 minutes. Remove from the heat, let rice cool slightly about 10 minutes. Mix in dill, mint, and lemon zest. (Blanched grape leaves and filling keep safely in a fridge for up to 36 hours.)

Place 1 blanched leaf smooth side down on counter with stem up. Remove the stem from base of leaf by slicing along both sides of stem to form thin triangle. Pat leaf dry using paper towels. Overlap cut ends of leaf to stop any filling from leaking out. Place heaping tablespoon filling ¼ inch from bottom of leaf where ends overlap. Fold bottom over filling and fold in sides. Roll leaf tightly around filling to create tidy roll. Replicate the process with the rest of the blanched leaves and filling.

Line 12-inch frying pan with one layer of remaining leaves. Place rolled leaves seam side down in tight rows in prepared skillet. Mix 1¼ cups water and lemon juice, put in to skillet, and bring to simmer over medium heat. Cover, decrease the heat to moderate to low, and simmer until water is almost completely absorbed and leaves and rice are tender and cooked through, forty to sixty minutes.

Move stuffed grape leaves to serving platter and allow it to cool to room temperature, approximately half an hour; discard leaves in skillet. Sprinkle with extra oil before you serve

Flavourful Calamari with Oranges

Servings: 8

Total time: 30 minutes

Ingredients

¼ cup olive oil

⅓ cup hazelnuts, skinned, and chopped

1 red bell pepper, stemmed seeded, and cut into 2-inch-long matchsticks

1 shallot, sliced thin

1 teaspoon Dijon mustard

2 celery ribs, sliced thin on bias

2 garlic cloves, minced

2 oranges

2 pounds squid, bodies sliced crosswise into ¼-inch-thick rings, tentacles halved

2 tablespoons baking soda

2½ tablespoons harissa

3 tablespoons chopped fresh mint

3 tablespoons red wine vinegar

Salt and pepper

Directions

Dissolve baking soda and 1 tablespoon salt in 3 cups cold water in large container. Submerge squid in brine, cover, put inside your fridge for about fifteen minutes. Remove squid from brine and separate bodies from tentacles.

Bring 8 cups water to boil in a big saucepan on moderate to high heat. Fill big container with ice water. Put in 2 tablespoons salt and tentacles to boiling water and cook for 30 seconds. Put in bodies and cook until bodies are firm and opaque throughout, about 90 seconds. Drain squid, move to ice water, and allow to sit until chilled, about 5 minutes.

Beat oil, vinegar, harissa, garlic, mustard, 1½ teaspoons salt, and ½ teaspoon pepper together in a big container. Drain squid well and put in to a container with dressing.

Cut away peel and pith from oranges. Quarter oranges, then slice crosswise into ½-inch-thick pieces. Put in oranges, bell pepper, celery, and shallot to squid and toss to coat. Cover and put in the fridge for minimum sixty minutes or up to 24 hours. Mix in hazelnuts and mint and sprinkle with salt and pepper to taste before you serve.

Fiery Red Whipped Feta

Servings: 2

Total time: 10 minutes

Ingredients

¼ teaspoon pepper

⅓ cup extra-virgin olive oil, plus extra for serving

½ teaspoon cayenne pepper

1 cup jarred roasted red peppers, rinsed, patted dry, and chopped

1 tablespoon lemon juice

8 ounces feta cheese, crumbled (2 cups)

Directions

Process feta, red peppers, oil, lemon juice, cayenne, and pepper using a food processor until smooth, approximately half a minute, scraping down sides of the container as required.

Move mixture to serving bowl, sprinkle with extra oil to taste, and serve. (Dip will keep safely in a fridge for up to 2 days; bring to room temperature before you serve.)

Flavourful Saffron Caulipeas

Servings: 8

Total time: 3 days 30 minutes

Ingredients

⅛ teaspoon saffron threads, crumbled

⅓ cup extra-virgin olive oil

½ head cauliflower (1 pound), cored and cut into 1-inch florets

½ lemon, sliced thin

1 cup canned chickpeas, rinsed

1 small sprig fresh rosemary

1 tablespoon minced fresh parsley

1½ teaspoons smoked paprika

1½ teaspoons sugar

2 tablespoons sherry vinegar

5 garlic cloves, peeled and smashed

Salt and pepper

Directions

Bring 2 quarts water to boil in a big saucepan. Put in cauliflower and 1 tablespoon salt and cook until florets start to become tender, approximately three minutes. Drain florets and move to paper towel–lined baking sheet.

Mix ¼ cup hot water and saffron in a container; set aside. Heat oil and garlic in small saucepan over moderate to low heat until aromatic and starting to sizzle but not brown, four to eight minutes. Mix in sugar, paprika, and rosemary and cook until aromatic, approximately half a minute. Remove from the heat, mix in saffron mixture, vinegar, 1½ teaspoons salt, and ¼ teaspoon pepper.

Mix florets, saffron mixture, chickpeas, and lemon in a big container. Cover and place in the fridge, stirring intermittently, for minimum 4 hours or for maximum 3 days. To serve, discard rosemary sprig, move cauliflower and chickpeas to serving bowl using a slotted spoon, and drizzle with parsley.

Flavourful Green-Black Olives

Servings: 8

Total time: 4 days 40 minutes

Ingredients

pepper flakes

½ teaspoon salt

¾ cup extra-virgin olive oil

1 cup brine-cured black olives with pits

1 cup brine-cured green olives with pits

1 garlic clove, minced

1 shallot, minced

2 teaspoons grated lemon zest

2 teaspoons minced fresh oregano

2 teaspoons minced fresh thyme

Directions

Wash olives comprehensively, then drain and pat dry using paper towels.

Toss olives with the rest of the ingredients in a container, cover, put inside your fridge for minimum 4 hours or for maximum 4 days. Allow to sit at room temperature for minimum half an hour before you serve.

Lunch Recipes

Grilled Chicken Salad with Fennel, Orange, and Raisins

Servings: 3

Total time: 1 hour 45 minutes

Ingredients:

- [ ] 1/4 cup extra virgin olive oil

- [ ] 1 tsp. Dijon mustard

- [ ] 1/2 lb. boneless, skinless chicken breast

- [ ] 1 Tbsp. freshly squeezed lemon juice

- [ ] 1/4 cup freshly squeezed orange juice

- [ ] 1 small fennel bulb, trimmed and chopped

- [ ] 1 Tbsp. minced fresh mint

- [ ] 1 tsp. Dijon mustard

- [ ] 1 1/2 Tbsp. golden raisins

- [ ] 2 1/2 Tbsp. warm water

- ☐   1 Boston Bibb lettuce, rinsed and spun dry

- ☐   1 small orange, peeled and divided into segments

- ☐   Sea salt

- ☐   Freshly ground black pepper

For the vinaigrette:

- ☐   1 Tbsp. balsamic vinegar

- ☐   3 Tbsp. extra virgin olive oil

Directions:

Blend the orange juice, lemon juice, mint, olive oil, and mustard in a bowl. Season to taste with salt and pepper.

Add the chicken breast in the mixture and turn several times to coat. Cover the bowl and refrigerate for at least an hour.

Take the bowl out of the refrigerator and set aside for 15 minutes.

Prepare the grill.

Soak the raisins in the warm water until plump.

Grill the chicken over medium high flame until cooked through, about 6 to 8 minutes per side depending on the thickness.

While the chicken is grilling, grill the fennel for about 6 minutes and the orange segments for about 3 minutes or until tender. Baste the chicken, fennel, and orange with the marinade all the time.

Transfer the grilled ingredients to a platter and set aside.

Place the lettuce and mint on a serving dish. Drain the raisins and set aside.

Prepare the vinaigrette by blending the balsamic vinegar and olive oil. Season with salt and pepper to taste.

Chop up the grilled chicken breast, fennel, and orange. Arrange on top of the lettuce, then scatter the raisins and drizzle the dressing on top. Serve right away.

Provençal Vegetable Soup

Servings: 3

Total time: 1 hour 55 minutes

Ingredients:

- ☐ 1/2 Tbsp. olive oil

- ☐ 1 small onion, chopped

- ☐ 1/2 cup chopped green beans

- ☐ 1/2 cup dry red beans

- ☐ 1/2 cup dry white beans

- ☐ 1 carrot, chopped

- ☐ 1 small zucchini, chopped

- ☐ 1/2 medium leek, trimmed and chopped

- ☐ 2 medium tomatoes

- ☐ 1 large potato, peeled and chopped

- ☐ 3 garlic cloves, minced

- ☐ 1 sage leaf

- ☐ 2 Tbsp. chopped fresh flat leaf parsley

- ☐ 1/2 cup whole wheat penne pasta

- ☐ Sea salt

- ☐ Freshly ground black pepper

For the Pesto:

- [ ] 3 garlic cloves

- [ ] 1/2 cup fresh basil, packed

- [ ] 2 Tbsp. olive oil

- [ ] 1/4 cup shredded Parmesan cheese

Directions:

1. Pour the red and white beans in a pot, then pour enough water to cover them by about an inch.

2. Place the pot over high flame, cover, and bring to a boil. Once boiling. Turn off the heat and set aside for an hour.

3. Prepare the pesto by combining the garlic, basil, cheese, and 1/2 tablespoon olive oil in the food processor. Pulse until pasty, then drizzle in the olive oil and blend until smooth. Refrigerate until ready to serve.

4. Ensure that the vegetables are all chopped in the same size.

5. Prepare the penne pasta based on the manufacturer's directions, then drain and toss in a bit of olive oil. Set aside.

6. Boil salted water in a small saucepan and blanch the tomatoes until tender. Immediately drain and plunge in a bowl of ice water. Skin the tomatoes, then remove the seeds and chop up. Set aside.

7. Place a soup pot over high flame and heat the olive oil. Sauté the onions until tender, then stir in the garlic, chopped tomatoes, and leek. Sauté until simmering and garlic is fragrant.

8. Add the red and white beans, green beans, zucchini, carrot, potato, parsley, and sage, then add just enough water to cover them. Bring to a boil, then reduce to low flame.

9. Cover the pot and simmer for 30 minutes, or until the vegetables are fork tender. If desired, puree the potatoes and mix into the soup.

10. Mix in the pasta, then season to taste with salt and pepper. Serve the soup with the pesto on the side.

Classic Niçoise Chicken

Servings: 4

Total time: 35 minutes

Ingredients:

- [ ] 2 lb chicken breasts or legs, excess skin and fat removed
- [ ] 3 Tbsp. extra virgin olive oil
- [ ] 2 small onions, chopped
- [ ] 1 garlic clove, minced
- [ ] 1/2 Tbsp. minced fresh thyme
- [ ] 3 ripe tomatoes, chopped
- [ ] 1/4 cup small black olives
- [ ] 1/4 cup vermouth or dry white wine
- [ ] 1/4 cup chopped fresh flat leaf parsley
- [ ] 2 Tbsp. freshly squeezed lemon juice
- [ ] Sea salt
- [ ] Freshly ground black pepper

Directions:

1. Season the chicken pieces all over with salt and pepper, then set aside.

2. Heat 1 1/2 tablespoons of oil in a heavy bottomed skillet over medium flame. Brown the chicken all over, approximately 6 minutes per side.

3. Meanwhile, place another skillet over medium flame and heat 1 1/2 tablespoons of olive oil.

4. Sauté the onion until tender, then stir in the garlic and sauté until golden. Stir in the parsley and thyme and sauté until fragrant. Turn off the heat and set aside.

5. Stir the tomatoes and vermouth or wine into the chicken pieces, scraping up the bottom to loosen any browned bits.

6. Set the flame to medium high, then simmer, uncovered, for about 15 to 20 minutes or until the sauce is thickened. The chicken must be cooked through.

7. Add the herb mixture in with the chicken, then mix well. Add the olives and lemon juice, then let everything boil for about 3 minutes.

8. Transfer the dish to a plate and serve right away.

Tunisian Turnovers with Tuna, Egg and Tomato

Servings: 2

Total time: 45 minutes

Ingredients:

☐ 2 pieces pita bread

☐ 2 Tbsp. extra virgin olive oil

☐ 5 oz. tuna packed in olive oil, drained

☐ 1 hard-boiled egg, sliced thinly

☐ 1 large ripe tomato, sliced thinly

☐ 1 small ripe tomato, diced

☐ 1 garlic clove, minced

☐ 1/4 small green bell pepper, seeded and minced

☐ 1/4 small yellow onion, minced

☐ 1/2 small English cucumber, sliced extra thin

- ☐ 1/4 cup pitted black olives

- ☐ 2 Tbsp. hot sauce

- ☐ 2 jarred pepperoncini peppers, drained and halved

- ☐ Sea salt

- ☐ Freshly ground black pepper

Directions:

Place a skillet over medium high flame and heat the olive oil. Saute the onion, tomato, garlic, and bell pepper until tender and simmering. Season to taste with salt and pepper, then turn off the heat.

Open up the pita bread and spoon the tomato sauce inside, then add cucumber slices, tuna, olives, pepperoncini pepper, and egg.

Arrange on a platter and server right away with hot sauce on the side.

Fish and Spinach Gratin

Servings: 3

Total time: 45 minutes

Ingredients:

- [ ] 1 Tbsp. extra virgin olive oil

- [ ] 3/4 lb firm white fish fillets

- [ ] 1 lb fresh spinach, rinsed thoroughly

- [ ] 1 small onion, chopped

- [ ] 1/2 Tbsp. Dijon mustard

- [ ] 1 small garlic clove, chopped

- [ ] 2 Tbsp. freshly squeezed lemon juice

- [ ] 1/3 cup ground dry unseasoned bread crumbs

- [ ] Sea salt

- [ ] Freshly ground black pepper

Directions:

1. Rinse the spinach thoroughly under cold running water.

2. Place a dry saucepan over medium flame and add the spinach. Cover and cook the spinach for about 8 minutes or until wilted. Remove from heat, chop, and set aside.

3. Wipe the saucepan clean and place it over medium low flame. Heat 1/2 tablespoon of olive oil and sauté the onion until tender. Add the garlic and sauté until fragrant.

4. Add the Dijon mustard and wilted spinach and sauté until thoroughly combined. Season with salt and pepper to taste. Turn off the heat and set aside.

5. Set the oven to 450 degrees F. Coat a small casserole or gratin dish with the remaining olive oil.

63

6. Wash the fish fillets thoroughly, then blot dry with paper towels and season both sides with salt and pepper.

7. Spread half of the spinach mixture on the dish in an even layer, then place the fish fillets on top. Sprinkle the lemon juice all over.

8. Add the remaining spinach mixture in an even layer on top, then sprinkle the bread crumbs all over.

9. Bake for 15 to 20 minutes, or until the fish is cooked through. Serve right away.

Calamari with Herb and Rice Stuffing

Servings: 6

Total time: 35 minutes

Ingredients:

- ☐   3 Tbsp. extra virgin olive oil

- ☐   3 cups vegetable or seafood broth

- ☐   1/3 cup uncooked short grain rice

- ☐   1 1/2 small yellow onions, minced

- ☐   1 1/2 lb. fresh spinach

- ☐   3 Tbsp. chopped fresh flat leaf parsley

- ☐   3 Tbsp. chopped fresh dill

- ☐   1 1/2 lb. baby squid

- ☐   1 1/2 tsp. sea salt

- ☐   Freshly ground black pepper

- ☐   Red chili flakes

Directions:

1. Place a large skillet over medium flame and heat 1 1/2 tablespoons of olive oil. Stir in the onion and sauté until tender and golden brown.

2. Stir in the parsley, dill, rice, and spinach, then season with salt, pepper, and red chili flakes. Simmer for about a minute, then turn off the heat. Let the mixture cool down slightly.

3. Remove the tentacles from the baby squid, then rinse the squid well. Stuff each squid with the rice mixture, then secure the ends with the toothpick. Ensure that there is space inside the squid for the rice to puff up later on.

4. Heat the rest of the olive oil in a skillet over medium flame, then add the calamari and cook until browned all over.

5. Pour the broth into the skillet, then cover and reduce to low flame. Simmer for up to 20 minutes, or until the rice inside the calamari is completely puffed and tender. Best served warm.

Grilled Lemon-Herb Chicken and Avocado Salad

Servings: 4

Total time: 40 minutes

Ingredients

Lemon-herb chicken

1 ½ pounds boneless, skinless chicken breasts

3 tablespoons of extra virgin olive oil

Zest and juice of 2 lemons

1 tablespoon chopped fresh oregano

1 tablespoon chopped dill

3 tablespoons fresh chopped parsley

Kosher salt and finely ground black pepper

Avocado salad

1 cup of barley

2 ½ cups of chicken broth

Zest and juice of 1 lemon

1 tablespoon whole grain mustard

1 tablespoon dried oregano

⅓ cup extra virgin olive oil

Kosher salt and finely ground black pepper

2 heads of red leaf lettuce

1 red onion sliced

1 pint of cherry tomatoes sliced

2 avocados sliced

Directions

Making the lemon herb chicken

1. Place the chicken in a large resealable plastic bag. In a medium bowl, whisk together the olive oil, lemon zest, lemon juice, oregano, dill, and parsley.

2. Pour marinade into the bag, seal it, and refrigerate for 30 minutes.

Making the salad

3. In a saucepan, bring in a chicken broth and barley to simmer over medium heat.

4. When it comes to simmer, cover the pot and cook until the barley is tender (40 minutes)

5. Drain and reserve it.

6. In a medium bowl, whisk together the lemon zest, mustard, oregano, and lemon juice. Gradually stream in the olive oil and whisk well to combine. Season with salt and pepper.

7. Prepare the grill for high heat. Remove chicken from the marinade and season with salt and pepper.

8. Grill the chicken until charred on both sides and fully cooked through by flipping it every 10 minutes. Remove chicken from the grill and reserve.

9. In a large bowl, toss the onions, tomatoes, and lettuce. Add the dressing and toss well to coat.

10. Slice the chicken and serve on top of the salad and next to avocado.

Tomato Salad with Grilled Halloumi and Herbs

Servings: 4

Total time: 15 minutes

Ingredients

1 pound of tomatoes, sliced into rounds

½ lemon

Flaky salt and finely ground pepper

Extra virgin olive oil

½ pound of halloumi cheese, sliced into 4 slabs

5 basil leaves, torn

2 tablespoons of finely chopped flat-leaf parsley

Directions

1. Preheat the grill or grill-pan over medium heat.

2. Arrange the tomatoes on a serving platter and squeeze lemon over them. Season with flaky salt and pepper.

3. Brush the grill grates with oil, then add the halloumi and cook, turning once until marks appear, and the cheese gets warmed throughout. This can take 1 minute on each side.

4. Place the halloumi on the tomatoes. Drizzle the salad with olive oil and sprinkle with basil and parsley.

5. Serve immediately

The Eggplant Pizza

Servings: 6

Total time: 25 minutes

Ingredients

1 large eggplant

⅓ cup olive oil

Salt and finely ground black pepper

1 ¼ marinara sauce

1 ½ shredded mozzarella cheese

2 cups cherry tomatoes, halved

½ cup torn basil leaves

Directions

1. Preheat the oven to 400 degrees Fahrenheit. Line a baking sheet with parchment paper.

2. Cut the ends off the eggplant. Then cut into ¾ inch thick slices. Arrange the slices on the prepared baking sheets, then brush each side of the slices with olive oil. Season with pepper and salt.

3. Roast the eggplants until nearly tender, 10 to 13 minutes

4. Remove trays from the oven and spread 2 tablespoons marinara sauce on top of each piece. Top generously with mozzarella and arrange 3 to 5 cherry tomatoes on top of each.

5. Return the pizzas to the oven and roast until cheese gets melted, and the tomatoes are blistered, 5 to 7 minutes more.

6. Serve the pizzas hot, garnished with basil

Salmon Bowl with Farro, Black Beans and Tahini Dressing

Servings: 1

Total time: 35 minutes

Ingredients

2 tablespoon of tahini

Zest and juice of 1 lemon

½ teaspoon of turmeric

¼ teaspoon of garlic powder

6 tablespoons of extra virgin oil

Kosher salt and finely ground black pepper

¼ cup farro

½ a cup of cooked black beans

½ teaspoon cumin

6 ounces' salmon

1 ½ teaspoons smoked paprika

4 Boston Lettuce leaves

½ Avocado thinly sliced

2 scallions thinly sliced

¼ Fresh chile, thinly sliced

Directions

1. In a small bowl, whisk together Tahini, lemon zest, lemon juice, ¼ spoon of turmeric, and garlic powder. Gradually add 3 tablespoons of the olive oil and whisk until the dressing is thick and well emulsified. Season with salt and pepper.

2. Bring the farro and 1 cup of water to simmer in a small pot over medium heat. Reduce the heat to low and simmer until the farro is tender, 20-25 minutes.

3. Combine the beans, 1 tablespoon of olive oil in a small bowl and put it aside.

4. Season the salmon with smoked paprika, coriander, remaining ¼ teaspoon turmeric, salt and pepper. Heat the remaining 2 tablespoons of olive oil in a medium-sized non-stick skillet over the medium heat. Add salmon and cook, undisturbed until brown on one side and just opaque in the center, about 5 minutes.

5. Place the lettuce leaves in the base of your serving bowl. Top with farro, black beans, and salmon. Garnish with avocado, scallions, and sliced chile.

6. Drizzle with dressing.

Dinners recipes

Harrisa Potato Salad

Servings: 7

Total time: 15 minutes

Ingredients

1 ½ pounds of baby potatoes

3 tablespoon of harissa paste

6 ounces of low-fat or non-fat Greek yogurt

¼ tablespoon of salt

¼ tablespoon of pepper

 2 lemon juice

¼ cup of finely diced red onion

¼ cup of fresh cilantro or parsley roughly chopped

Directions

1. Keep the potatoes in a big pot and cover them with 1 to 3 inches of salted water. Boil water over medium-high heat. Cook potatoes uncovered until they are fork-tender, about 12 minutes. Drain the potatoes and set them aside to wet.

2. In a small bowl whisk the harissa, Greek yogurt, salt, pepper, and lemon juice together.

3. Transfer the still warm potatoes to a bi bowl. Fold it in gently until potatoes are well coated together. Then carefully cover in the diced red onions and herbs.

4. Serve immediately while it is still warm

Greek Lemon Chicken Soup

Servings: 6

Total time: 15 minutes

Ingredients

3 tbsp olive oil

1 pound boneless chicken thighs cut into 1-5-inch chunks

Kosher salt with fine black pepper

4 cloves garlic,

1 onion

3 carrots, peeled and diced

3 stalks celer

½ teaspoon dried thyme

8 cups chicken stalk

2 bay leaves

2 cans of cannellini beans, rinsed and drained

4 cups baby spinach

2 tablespoons freshly squeezed lemon juice

2 tablespoons chopped fresh parsley leaves

2 tablespoons chopped fresh dill

Directions

1. Heat 1 tablespoon of olive oil in a stockpot over medium heat. Season chicken thighs with salt and pepper, to taste. Add chicken to the stockpot and cook until golden, about 2-3 minutes set aside.

2. Add remaining one tablespoon oil to the stockpot. Add garlic, onion, celery, and carrots. Cook, occasionally stirring, until tender for about 3-4 minutes. Stir in thyme until fragrant.

3. Whisk in the chicken stock and bay leaves. Bring to boil. Reduce the heat and bring in the cannellini beans and chicken. Stir occasionally until slightly thickened.

4. Stir in spinach until wilted, about 2 minutes. Stir in lemon juice, parsley, and dill; season with salt and pepper to taste.

5. Serve immediately.

Walnut-Rosemary Crusted Salmon

Servings: 4

Total time: 30 minutes

Ingredients:

2 teaspoons of Dijon mustard

1 minced clove garlic

¼ teaspoon of lemon zest

½ teaspoon of honey

½ teaspoon of kosher salt

1 teaspoon of chopped fresh rosemary

3 tablespoons of panko breadcrumbs

¼ teaspoon of crushed red pepper

3 tablespoons of finely chopped walnuts

1 pound of frozen or fresh skinless salmon fillet

1 teaspoon of extra-virgin olive oil

Olive oil

Directions:

Preheat the oven to 420°F and use parchment paper to line a rimmed baking sheet.

Combine mustard, lemon zest, garlic, lemon juice, honey, rosemary, crushed red pepper, and salt in a bowl.

Combine walnuts and panko, with oil, in another bowl.

Place the salmon on that baking sheet. Spread that mustard mix on the fish, along with the panko mix. Make sure the fish is adequately coated with the mixtures. Spray olive oil lightly on the salmon.

Bake for about 8-12 minutes (till the salmon can be separated using a fork).

Greek Yogurt Chicken Salad Stuffed Peppers

Servings: 6

Total time: 15 minutes

Ingredients

⅔ cup greek yogurt

2 tablespoons Dijon mustard

2 tablespoons seasoned vinegar

Kosher salt and freshly ground black pepper

⅓ cup chopped fresh parsley

Meat from 1 rotisserie chicken, cubed

4 stalks celery sliced

1 bunch scallions, sliced and divided

1 pint cherry tomatoes, quartered and divided

½ English cucumber diced

3 bell peppers halved and seeds removed

Directions

1. In a medium bowl, whisk together the Greek yogurt, mustard and rice vinegar, season with salt and pepper. Stir in parsley.

2. Add the chicken, celery, and ¾ of each of the scallions, tomatoes, and cucumbers. Stir well to combine.

3. Divide the chicken salad among the bell pepper halves.

4. Garnish the remaining scallions, tomatoes, and cucumbers.

Greek Salad Nachos

Servings: 6

Total time: 30 minutes

Ingredients:

A ⅓ cup of hummus

2 tablespoons of extra-virgin olive oil

1 tablespoon of lemon juice

¼ teaspoon of ground pepper

3 cups of whole-grain pita chips

1 cup of chopped lettuce

A ½ cup of quartered grape tomatoes

A ¼ cup of crumbled feta cheese

2 tablespoons of chopped olives

2 tablespoons of minced red onion

1 tablespoon of minced fresh oregano

Directions:

Whisk pepper, lemon juice, oil, and hummus in a bowl.

Spread the pita chips on a plate in one layer.

Cover the chips with about ¾ of that hummus mix and top it with tomatoes, red onion, olives, feta, and lettuce. Cover it with the rest of the hummus. Sprinkle oregano on top before serving it.

Caprese Stuffed Portobello Mushrooms

Servings: 4

Total time: 65 minutes

Ingredients:

3 tablespoons of divided extra-virgin olive oil

1 medium minced clove garlic

½ teaspoon of salt

½ teaspoon of ground pepper

About 14 ounces of Portobello mushrooms, with gills and stems, removed

1 cup of halved cherry tomatoes

A ½ cup of fresh and drained mozzarella pearls patted dry

A ½ cup of thinly sliced fresh basil

2 teaspoons of balsamic vinegar

Directions:

Preheat the oven to 400°F. Combine a ¼ teaspoon of salt, two tablespoons of oil, and a ¼ teaspoon of pepper in a bowl. Use a brush for coating the mushrooms with this mixture.

Place the mushrooms on a baking sheet and bake it for about ten minutes (till the mushrooms get soft).

Stir basil, tomatoes, and mozzarella in a pan. Mix 1 tablespoon of oil, a ¼ teaspoon of salt, and a ¼ teaspoon of pepper in a bowl.

Remove the components of the pan after the mushrooms soften. Fill the mushrooms with the tomato mix.

Bake till the tomatoes wilt and the cheese melts, for about 15 minutes. Drizzle the mushrooms with half teaspoons of vinegar before serving.

Chicken in Tomato-Balsamic Pan Sauce

Servings: 4

Total time: 70 minutes

Ingredients:

2 8-ounce skinless, boneless chicken breasts

½ teaspoon of salt

½ teaspoon of ground pepper

A ¼ cup of white whole-wheat flour

3 tablespoons of extra-virgin olive oil

A ½ cup of halved cherry tomatoes

2 tablespoons of sliced shallot

A ¼ cup of balsamic vinegar

1 cup of low-sodium chicken broth

1 tablespoon of minced garlic

1 tablespoon of toasted and crushed fennel seeds

1 tablespoon of butter

Directions:

Slice the chicken breasts into 4 pieces and beat them with a mallet till it reaches a thickness of a ¼ inch. Use ¼ teaspoons of pepper and salt to coat the chicken.

Heat two tablespoons of oil in a skillet and keep the heat to a medium. Cook the chicken breasts for two minutes on each side. Transfer it to a serving plate and cover it with foil to keep it warm.

Add one tablespoon oil, shallot, and tomatoes in a pan and cook till it softens. Add vinegar and boil the mix till the vinegar gets reduced by half. Put fennel seeds, garlic, salt, and pepper and cook for about four minutes. Remove it from the heat and stir it with butter.

Pour this sauce over chicken and serve.

Greek Chicken with Lemon Vinaigrette and Roasted Spring Vegetables

Servings: 4

Total time: 80 minutes

Ingredients:

For the lemon vinaigrette

1 lemon

1 tablespoon olive oil

1 tablespoon crumbled feta cheese

½ teaspoon honey

For the Greek Chicken and roasted veggies

8 ounce of boneless, skinless chicken breast, cut lengthwise in half

A ¼ cup of light mayonnaise

6 cloves of minced garlic

A ½ cup of panko bread crumbs

3 tablespoons of grated Parmesan cheese

½ teaspoon of kosher salt

½ teaspoon of black pepper

1-inch pieces of asparagus, 2 cups

1½ cups of sliced cremini mushrooms

1½ cups of halved cherry tomatoes

1 tablespoon of olive oil

Directions:

To make the vinaigrette, put half teaspoons of zest, one tablespoon of lemon juice, olive oil, cheese, and honey in a bowl.

For the vegetables and chicken, preheat the oven to 470°F. Use a meat mallet for flattening the chicken between two pieces of plastic wrap.

Place the chicken in a bowl and add two garlic cloves and mayonnaise. Mix cheese, bread crumbs, a ¼ teaspoon of pepper, and a ¼ teaspoon of salt together. Dip the chicken in this crumb mix. Spray olive oil over the chicken.

Roast in the oven till the chicken is done and vegetables are tender. Sprinkle dill over it and serve.

Caprese Chicken Hasselback style

Servings: 4

Total time: 75 minutes

Ingredients:

2 skinless, boneless chicken breasts - 8 ounces each

½ teaspoon of salt

½ teaspoon of ground pepper

1 medium tomato, sliced

3 ounces of fresh mozzarella, halved and sliced

A ¼ cup of prepared pesto

8 cups of broccoli florets

2 tablespoons of olive oil

Directions:

Preheat the oven to 375°F and coat a rimmed baking sheet with cooking spray.

Make crosswire cuts at half inches in the chicken breasts. Sprinkle pepper and salt on them. Fill the cuts with mozzarella slices and tomato alternatively. Brush both the chicken breasts with pesto and put it on the baking sheet.

Mix broccoli, oil, salt, and pepper in a bowl. Put in the tomatoes if there are any left. Put this mixture on one side of the baking sheet.

Bake till the broccoli is tender, and the chicken is not pink in the center. Cut each of the breasts in half and serve.

Chicken Souvlaki Kebabs with Couscous

Servings: 4

Total time: 2 hours 65 minutes

Ingredients:

For the Kebabs-

1 pound of boneless, skinless chicken breast halves in ½-inch strips

1 cup of sliced fennel

⅓ Cup of dry white wine

A ¼ cup of lemon juice

3 tablespoons of canola oil

4 cloves of garlic, minced

2 teaspoons dried and crushed oregano

½ teaspoon salt

¼ teaspoon black pepper

Couscous

1 teaspoon of olive oil

A ½ cup of Israeli couscous

1 cup of water

A ½ cup of snipped dried tomatoes

A ¾ cup of chopped red sweet pepper

½ cup each of chopped cucumber and red onion

⅓ Cup of plain fat-free Greek yogurt

A ¼ cup of fresh basil leaves, thinly sliced

A ¼ cup of snipped fresh parsley

1 tablespoon of lemon juice

¼ teaspoon of salt

¼ teaspoon of black pepper

Directions:

Place chicken with sliced fennel in a sealable plastic bag and set aside. Combine the lemon juice, white wine, oil, oregano, garlic, pepper, and salt in a bowl for the marinade. Take a ¼ cup of this marinade and set aside.

Pour rest of the marinade over the chicken and refrigerate for 1 ½ hour.

Take wooden skewers and thread chicken on to it in accordion style.

Grill the chicken skewers for six to eight minutes.

Put all the ingredients of couscous in a pan and cook it in olive oil. Serve it alongside the chicken.

Vegan/vegetarian recipes

Grilled Vegetable and Feta Cheese Salad

Servings: 4

Total time: 15 minutes

Ingredients:

1 Medium Yellow Squash

1 Medium Eggplant

1 Medium Zucchini

1 1/2 cup of Mixed Greens

25-30 Green String Beans

1 cup of Crumbled Feta Cheese

1 cup of Pitted & Halved Kalamata Olives

1/2 cup of Chopped Fresh Parsley

1 Large Yellow Onion

2 tablespoons of Lemon Juice

3/4 cup of Extra-Virgin Olive Oil

Pepper

Salt

Directions:

1. Cut your squash, eggplant, and zucchini into 1/2-inch thick slices.

2. Peel your onion and cut it into 1/2-inch thick slices.

3. Brush your vegetables with olive oil. Season your vegetables with salt and pepper. Set the vegetables to the side.

4. Gently steam your string beans, drain and set to the side.

5. Place your vegetables (not your string beans) on your grill and cook for 6 to 7 minutes until they are tender. Place your cooked vegetables on a plate and allow to cool. Once cool, cut them into 1/2-inch pieces. Cut your string beans into 1/2-inch pieces.

6. Place all your vegetables (including the parsley and greens) into a large-sized bowl. Add your lemon juice, olives, feta cheese, and the rest of your olive oil. Add salt and pepper. Toss all your ingredients together.

7. Serve and Enjoy!

Dumplings

Servings: 6

Total time: 55 minutes

Ingredients:

3 medium zucchini, spiralized

3.5-ounce fresh spinach

1/3 cup almond flour

2 1/2 tablespoons coconut flour

1/2 teaspoon sea salt

1/2 teaspoon cracked black pepper

1/16 teaspoon ground nutmeg

3 tablespoons olive oil

2 medium eggs, pasture raised

8.8-ounce ricotta cheese, full-fat

1/2 cup grated Parmesan cheese, full-fat

3 cups tomato pasta sauce, unsweetened

Directions:

Set oven to 350 degrees F and let preheat.

In the meantime, blanch spinach in boiling water for 30 seconds or until leaves wilt and let cool.

Then pat dry to remove excess moisture from spinach and chop and place in a bowl.

Add remaining ingredients except for zucchini and pasta sauce and stir until well mixed.

Shape mixture into 18 small dumpling balls, each about 2 teaspoons.

Take a heatproof dish, pour in tomato sauce and arrange dumpling in it.

Drizzle oil over dumpling and place baking dish into the oven to bake for 35 to 40 minutes or until top is nicely browned.

Serve dumpling with spiralized zucchini noodles.

Garlic & Vegetable Calzone

Servings: 2

Total time: 45 minutes

Ingredients:

3 Asparagus Stalks (Cut In 1-Inch Pieces)

1/2 cup of Chopped Broccoli

1/2 cup of Chopped Spinach

2 teaspoons of Olive Oil

2 tablespoons of Minced Garlic

1/2 cup of Sliced Mushrooms

1 Medium Sliced Tomato

1/2 pound of Frozen Whole-Wheat Bread Dough (Thawed)

1/2 cup of Shredded Mozzarella Cheese

2/3 cup of Pizza Sauce

Directions:

1. Preheat your oven to 400 degrees. Lightly coat your baking sheet with cooking spray.

2. In a medium bowl, add your spinach, asparagus, mushrooms, garlic, and broccoli. Drizzle 1 teaspoon of your olive oil over your vegetables and toss them together to mix.

3. Heat a large frying pan over a medium-high heat. Add your vegetables and saute for approximately 4 to 5 minutes. Stir frequently. Remove from the heat and allow to cool.

4. On a floured surface, cut your bread dough in half. Press each of your halves into a circle. Use a rolling pin and roll your dough into an oval shape. On one 1/2 of the oval, add 1/2 of your sauteed vegetables, 1/2 of your tomato slices, and 1/4 cup of your cheese. Wet your finger and rub the edge of your dough that has your filling

on it. Fold your dough over the filling and press your edges together. Roll your edges and press down with a fork. Place your calzone on your baking sheet. Repeat process to make the other calzone.

5. Brush your calzones with your remaining teaspoon of olive oil. Bake for 20 minutes until golden brown.

6. Heat your pizza sauce in your microwave. Place each of your calzones on a plate. Each one gets a 1/3 cup of pizza sauce. You can place it on the side or pour it on top of the calzone.

7. Serve and Enjoy!

Roasted Brussels Sprouts

Servings: 5

Total time: 15 minutes

Ingredients:

1-pound Brussels sprout

1 teaspoon minced garlic

1 tablespoon minced parsley

1/2 teaspoon salt

1/4 teaspoon cracked black pepper

3 tablespoons olive oil

2 teaspoons lemon juice

1 tablespoon lemon zest

1 tablespoon mustard paste

2 tablespoons grated parmesan cheese, full-fat

Directions:

Trim Brussels sprout, rinse well, then cut into quarters and let rest for 5 minutes.

Take a steamer, fill with 1-inch water, add sprouts and let steam for 8 to 10 minutes or until tender.

In the meantime, place remaining ingredients except for cheese and lemon zest in a large bowl and stir until combined.

Add steamed sprouts and toss until well coated.

Top with cheese and lemon zest and serve.

Cauliflower Parmesan Soup

Servings: 6

Total time: 40 minutes

Ingredients:

1 medium head of cauliflower, florets chopped

1/2 of medium white onion, peeled and sliced

½ of medium leek, sliced

4 tablespoons unsalted butter

¾ teaspoon salt

½ teaspoon cracked black pepper

2 tablespoons fresh thyme, chopped

4 tablespoons olive oil

1 cup grated parmesan cheese, full-fat

2 cups vegetable broth

3 cups water

Directions:

Place a large pot over medium heat, add 2 tablespoons butter and cook until melt completely.

Then add onion, leek, and salt and cook for 3 to 5 minutes or until softened.

Add half of the chopped cauliflower florets, oil, vegetable broth, and water and stir until mixed.

Bring the mixture to simmer and cook for 15 minutes or until cauliflower is tender.

Stir in a ¾ portion of remaining cauliflower florets into the pot and continue simmering until tender.

In the meantime, place a frying pan over medium heat, add remaining butter, remaining chopped cauliflower florets and thyme and cook for 3 to 5 minutes or until butter starts to bubble, and cauliflower is nicely golden brown.

When cauliflower is cook, remove the pot from heat and blend with a stick blender until smooth.

Top soup with browned cauliflower and serves.

Braised Fennel with Lemon

Servings: 2

Total time: 1 hour and 50 minutes

Ingredients:

2 pounds fennel bulbs

¾ pound lemons

1 teaspoon minced garlic

1 ½ teaspoon sea salt

¾ teaspoon cracked black pepper

2 teaspoons fresh rosemary, chopped

1 teaspoon fresh thyme, chopped

6 tablespoons apple cider vinegar

1/4 cup olive oil

Directions:

Set oven to 375 degrees F and let preheat.

In the meantime, slice fennel bulb into wedges, slice lemons into thin wedges and arrange in a large baking dish in a single layer.

Whisk together garlic, rosemary, thyme, vinegar, and oil until combined, pour this mixture evenly over vegetables in the baking dish, season with salt and black pepper and cover with aluminum foil.

Place this baking dish into the heated oven and bake for 1 hour, then uncover baking dish and continue baking for 30 to 40 minutes or until vegetables are roasted and crispy.

Serve straight away with baked chicken.

Cauliflower Mash

Servings: 4

Total time: 25 minutes

Ingredients:

2 pounds cauliflower florets

1 teaspoon minced garlic

1 teaspoon salt

½ teaspoon cracked black pepper

½ teaspoon red pepper flakes

½ teaspoon turmeric powder

1 teaspoon lemon zest

2 tablespoons unsalted butter

1 teaspoon olive oil

¼ cup Greek yogurt

Directions:

Fill a large pot half-full with water and bring to boil over medium-high heat.

Add cauliflower florets and boil for 15 minutes or until tender.

Then drain cauliflower florets well, return to pot and add garlic, butter, oil, and yogurt.

Blend the mixture using a stick blender until smooth, then add salt, black pepper, turmeric, and red pepper flakes and continue blending until fluffy.

Stir in lemon zest and serve immediately.

Ginger And Butternut Bisque Yum

Servings: 6

Total time: 28 minutes

Ingredients

1 cup of diced yellow onion

4 minced cloves of garlic

2 teaspoon of peeled and chopped ginger

1 cup of chopped carrot

1 green apple chopped

1 peeled and chopped butternut squash

1 teaspoon salt

2 cups of water

¼ cup of finely chopped parsley

Black pepper

Directions

Prepare the ingredients accordingly and keep them on the side

Add onions and cook for minutes

Add just a splash of water . Add garlic, carrot, ginger, apple, squash, and salt

Give it a nice stir. Add water and lock up the lid

Cook on HIGH pressure for 5 minutes. Naturally, release the pressure

Allow it to cool for 15 minutes

Blend the soup in batches, or you may use an immersion blender as well to blend in the pot until it is creamy. Add parsley and season with some black pepper. Serve and enjoy!

Roasted Broccoli

Servings: 4

Total time: 20 minutes

Ingredients:

4 cups broccoli florets

10 pitted black olives, sliced

1 teaspoon minced garlic

¼ teaspoon salt

1 teaspoon dried oregano

½ teaspoon lemon zest

1 tablespoon lemon juice

1 tablespoon olive oil

Directions:

Set oven to 450 degrees F and let preheat.

In the meantime, place broccoli florets in a bowl, add garlic, salt, oil and toss until evenly coated.

Spread this mixture in a single layer on a baking sheet and place into the heated oven.

Bake for 12 to 15 minutes or until broccoli florets are tender and nicely golden brown.

While broccoli cook, stir together olives, lemon zest, and lemon juice.

When vegetables are done, transfer them to a serving dish, add olive mixture and stir until combined.

Serve straightaway.

Dessert Recipes

Pistachio Ice-Cream

Servings: 6

Total time: 30 minutes

Ingredients:

2 cups whole milk

1 cup unsalted pistachios, finely ground

¾ cup sugar, divided

½ teaspoon vanilla extract

5 egg yolks

½ cup whole pistachios

1½ cups heavy cream

Directions:

In a pan, add all the milk, ground pistachios and ¼ cup of the sugar and bring to a boil, stirring frequently.

Stir in the vanilla extract and remove from the heat.

In a bowl, add the remaining sugar and egg yolks and beat well.

With a ladle, add some hot milk, stirring continuously until well combined.

Add the egg yolk mixture into the pan and mix well.

Place the pan over medium-low heat and cook for about 7-10 minutes, stirring frequently.

Remove from the heat and through a strainer, strain the mixture into a bowl.

Refrigerate the bowl for about 2 hours.

Remove from the refrigerator and stir in the heavy cream and whole pistachios.

Transfer the mixture into an ice cream maker and process according to the manufacturer's directions.

Now, transfer the mixture into an airtight container and freeze for about 2 hours before serving.

Fruity Yogurt Parfait

Servings: 4

Total time: 30 minutes

Ingredients:

2 cups plain Greek yogurt

¼ cup honey

¼ cup water

2 tablespoons sugar

½ teaspoon fresh lime zest, grated finely

¼ teaspoon ground cinnamon

¼ teaspoon vanilla extract

2 peaches, pitted and quartered

4 plums, pitted and quartered

¼ cup almonds, toasted and chopped

Directions:

In a bowl, add the yogurt and honey and mix until well combined.

Set aside.

In a pan, mix together the remaining ingredients except the almonds over medium heat and cook for about 8-10 minutes or until fruits becomes tender, stirring occasionally.

Remove from the heat and set aside at room temperature to cool.

Divide half of the yogurt mixture into 4 tall serving glasses evenly.

Divide the fruit mixture over yogurt evenly and top each with the remaining yogurt.

Garnish with almonds and serve.

Roasted Pears

Servings: 6

Total time: 40 minutes

Ingredients:

¼ cup pear nectar

3 tablespoons honey

2 tablespoons butter, melted

1 teaspoon fresh orange zest, grated

3 ripe medium Bosc pears, peeled and cored

½ cup mascarpone cheese

2 tablespoons powdered sugar

1/3 cup salted pistachios, chopped

Directions:

Preheat the oven to 400 degrees F.

In a bowl, add the pear nectar, honey, butter and orange zest and mix well.

In a 2-quart rectangular baking dish, arrange the pears, cut sides down and top with the honey mixture.

Roast for about 20-25 minutes, spooning liquid over pears occasionally.

Remove from the oven and transfer the pears onto serving plates with some of the cooking liquid.

In a bowl, add the mascarpone cheese and powdered sugar and mix well.

Top the pears with the cheese mixture and serve with the garnishing of pistachios.

Chocolate Mousse

Servings: 4

Total time: 20 minutes

Ingredients:

3½ ounces dark chocolate, chopped

¾ cup milk

1 tablespoon honey

½ teaspoon vanilla extract

2 cups plain Greek yogurt

2 tablespoons fresh raspberries

1 tablespoon chocolate shaving

Directions:

In a pan, add the chocolate and milk over medium-low heat and cook for about 3-5 minutes or until chocolate melts, stirring continuously.

Add the honey and vanilla extract and stir to combine well.

Remove from the heat and set aside at room temperature to cool slightly.

In a large glass bowl, place the yogurt and chocolate mixture and gently, stir to combine.

Refrigerate to chill for about 2 hours.

Serve with the topping of the raspberries and chocolate shaving.

Tahini Cookies

Servings: 30

Total time: 35 minutes

Ingredients:

1½ cups whole-wheat pastry flour

1 tablespoon baking soda

Pinch of salt

¾ cup sugar

½ cup butter, softened

½ cup tahini

1 tablespoon orange blossom water

1 tablespoon honey

1 medium egg

Directions:

In a large bowl, mix together the flour, baking soda and salt.

In the bowl of a stand mixer, add the sugar and butter and beat on medium-high speed until light and fluffy.

Add the tahini and beat well.

Add the orange blossom water and honey and beat until well combined.

Add the egg and beat on low speed until well combined.

Slowly, add the flour mixture, mixing well until a dough form.

With a plastic wrap, cover the bowl and refrigerate for about 1 hour.

Preheat the oven to 350 degrees F. Line 2 baking sheets with parchment paper.

With 2 tablespoons of dough, make balls and arrange onto the prepared baking sheets about 3-inch apart.

With the back of a lightly, floured fork, gently flatten each ball.

Bake for about 13-15 minutes or until golden brown.

Remove from the oven and place the baking sheets onto the wire racks for about 5 minutes.

Carefully, invert the cookies onto the wire racks to cool completely before serving.

Chocolate Muffins

Servings: 6

Total time: 30 minutes

Ingredients

½ cup buckwheat flour

½ cup almond flour

4 tbsp. arrowroot powder

4 tbsp. cacao powder

1 tsp. Baking powder

½ tsp. bicarbonate soda

½ cup boiled water

1/3 cup maple syrup

1/3 cup coconut oil, melted

1 tbsp. apple cider vinegar

½ cup unsweetened dark chocolate chips

Directions

Preheat your oven to 350°F.

Line 6 cups of a muffin tin with paper liners.

Place the flours, arrowroot powder, baking powder, and bicarbonate of soda and mix well in a bowl.

In a separate bowl, place the boiled water, maple syrup, and coconut oil and beat until well combined.

Place the flour mixture and mix until just combined. Gently fold in the chocolate chips.

Transfer the mixture into prepared muffin cups evenly.

Bake for about 20 minutes, or until a toothpick inserted in the center comes out clean.

Remove the muffin tin from the oven and place onto a wire rack to cool for about 10 minutes to cool.

Serve and enjoy.

Baklava

Servings: 18

Total time: 70 minutes

Ingredients:

1 pound nuts (pistachios, almonds, walnuts), chopped

1 teaspoon ground cinnamon

1 (16-ounce) package phyllo dough

1 cup butter, melted

1 cup white sugar

1 cup water

½ cup honey

1 teaspoon vanilla extract

Directions:

Preheat the oven to 350 degrees F. Grease a 9x13-inch baking dish.

In a bowl, add the nuts and cinnamon and toss to coat well.

Set aside.

Unroll the phyllo dough and cut in half.

Arrange 2 dough sheets into the prepared baking dish and coat with some butter.

Repeat with 8 dough sheets in layers and sprinkle with 2-3 tablespoons of nut mixture.

Repeat with remaining dough sheets, butter and nuts.

With a sharp knife, cut into diamond shapes all the way to the bottom of the baking dish.

Bake for about 50 minutes or until top becomes golden and crisp.

Meanwhile, for sauce: in a pan, add the sugar and water and cook until sugar is melted, stirring continuously.

Stir in the honey and vanilla extract and simmer for about 20 minutes.

Remove the baklava from oven and immediately place the sauce on top evenly.

Set aside to cool before serving.

Blueberry Muffins

Servings: 8

Total time: 30 minutes

Ingredients

1 cup buckwheat flour

¼ cup arrowroot starch

1½ tsp. Baking powder

¼ tsp. sea salt

2 eggs

½ cup unsweetened almond milk

3 tbsp. maple syrup

2 tbsp. coconut oil, melted

1 cup fresh blueberries

Directions

Preheat your oven to 350°F and line 8 cups of a muffin tin.

In a bowl, place the buckwheat flour, arrowroot starch, baking powder, and salt, and mix well.

In a separate bowl, place the eggs, almond milk, maple syrup, and coconut oil, and beat until well combined.

Pour in the flour mixture and mix until just combined.

Gently, fold in the blueberries. Transfer the mixture into prepared muffin cups evenly. Bake for about 25 minutes or until a toothpick inserted in the center comes out clean.

Remove the muffin tin from the oven and place onto a wire rack to cool for about 10 minutes.

Serve and enjoy.

Cinnamon Apple Chips

Servings: 4

Total time: 2 hours 10 minutes

Ingredients

Cooking spray

2 tsp. cinnamon powder

2 apples, cored and thinly sliced

Directions

Arrange apple slices on a lined baking sheet, then spray them with cooking oil

Sprinkle cinnamon and put them in the oven and bake at 300 ☐ F for 2 hours.

Divide into bowls and serve as a snack.

Enjoy!

21-day Meal Plan

Day 1

Breakfast- Greek Yogurt Breakfast Parfaits with Roasted Grapes

Lunch- Grilled Chicken Salad with Fennel, Orange, and Raisins

Dinner- Harrisa Potato Salad

Day 2

Breakfast- Pome-9granate Cherry Smoothie Bowl

Lunch-Provençal Vegetable Soup

Dinner- Greek Lemon Chicken Soup

Day 3

Breakfast- Quickie Honey Nut Granola

Lunch-Classic Niçoise Chicken

Dinner- Walnut-Rosemary Crusted Salmon

Day 4

Breakfast- Mashed Chickpea, Feta, and Avocado Toast

Lunch-Tunisian Turnovers with Tuna, Egg and Tomato

Dinner- Greek Yogurt Chicken Salad Stuffed Peppers

Day 5

Breakfast- Baked Ricotta with Pears

Lunch-Fish and Spinach Gratin

Dinner- Greek Salad Nachos

Day 6

Breakfast- Breakfast Polenta

Lunch-Calamari with Herb and Rice Stuffing

Dinner- Caprese Stuffed Portobello Mushrooms

Day 7

Breakfast- Scrambled Eggs with Goat Cheese and Roasted Peppers

Lunch-Grilled Lemon-Herb Chicken and Avocado Salad

Dinner- Chicken in Tomato-Balsamic Pan Sauce

Day 8

Breakfast- Greek Yogurt Breakfast Parfaits with Roasted Grapes

Lunch- Grilled Chicken Salad with Fennel, Orange, and Raisins

Dinner- Harrisa Potato Salad

Day 9

Breakfast- Pome-9granate Cherry Smoothie Bowl

Lunch-Provençal Vegetable Soup

Dinner- Greek Lemon Chicken Soup

Day 10

Breakfast- Quickie Honey Nut Granola

Lunch-Classic Niçoise Chicken

Dinner- Walnut-Rosemary Crusted Salmon

Day 11

Breakfast- Mashed Chickpea, Feta, and Avocado Toast

Lunch-Tunisian Turnovers with Tuna, Egg and Tomato

Dinner- Greek Yogurt Chicken Salad Stuffed Peppers

Day 12

Breakfast- Baked Ricotta with Pears

Lunch-Fish and Spinach Gratin

Dinner- Greek Salad Nachos

Day 13

Breakfast- Breakfast Polenta

Lunch-Calamari with Herb and Rice Stuffing

Dinner- Caprese Stuffed Portobello Mushrooms

Day 14

Breakfast- Scrambled Eggs with Goat Cheese and Roasted Peppers

Lunch-Grilled Lemon-Herb Chicken and Avocado Salad

Dinner- Chicken in Tomato-Balsamic Pan Sauce

Day 15

Breakfast- Greek Yogurt Breakfast Parfaits with Roasted Grapes

Lunch- Grilled Chicken Salad with Fennel, Orange, and Raisins

Dinner- Harrisa Potato Salad

Day 16

Breakfast- Pome-9granate Cherry Smoothie Bowl

Lunch-Provençal Vegetable Soup

Dinner- Greek Lemon Chicken Soup

Day 17

Breakfast- Quickie Honey Nut Granola

Lunch-Classic Niçoise Chicken

Dinner- Walnut-Rosemary Crusted Salmon

Day 18

Breakfast- Mashed Chickpea, Feta, and Avocado Toast

Lunch-Tunisian Turnovers with Tuna, Egg and Tomato

Dinner- Greek Yogurt Chicken Salad Stuffed Peppers

Day 19

Breakfast- Baked Ricotta with Pears

Lunch-Fish and Spinach Gratin

Dinner- Greek Salad Nachos

Day 20

Breakfast- Breakfast Polenta

Lunch-Calamari with Herb and Rice Stuffing

Dinner- Caprese Stuffed Portobello Mushrooms

Day 21

Breakfast- Scrambled Eggs with Goat Cheese and Roasted Peppers

Lunch-Grilled Lemon-Herb Chicken and Avocado Salad

Dinner- Chicken in Tomato-Balsamic Pan Sauce

Conclusion

Changing your behavior leads to healthy habits that can help you lose weight in the long run. The Noom app is a gift for bringing desirable lifestyle changes through constant motivation, provision for tracking, and education. It has gained popularity in recent times. Check with your health specialist and see if you can use this program. I am sure that it will bring you lasting results just like others!

9 781914 276095